Espresso for a
Woman's Spirit

Espresso for a Woman's Spirit

Encouraging Stories of Hope and Humor

PAM VREDEVELT

Multnomah Publishers® *Sisters, Oregon*

ESPRESSO FOR A WOMAN'S SPIRIT
Encouraging Stories of Hope and Humor
published by Multnomah Publishers, Inc.

© 2000 by Pam Vredevelt
International Standard Book Number 1-57673-636-9

Cover art by Michael Crampton/Mendola Ltd.

Unless otherwise noted, Scripture quotations are taken from *The Holy Bible,*
New International Version (NIV) © 1973, 1984 by International Bible Society.
Used by permission of Zondervan Publishing House.
Also quoted: *The Message* (MSG) © 1993 by Eugene H. Peterson
The Living Bible (TLB) © 1971. Used by permission of Tyndale House Publishers, Inc. All rights reserved.
The Holy Bible, King James Version (KJV).
Holy Bible, New Living Translation (NLT) © 1996.
Used by permission of Tyndale House Publishers, Inc. All rights reserved.
The New Testament in Modern English, Revised Edition (PHP) © 1958, 1960, 1972 by J. B. Phillips
The Amplified Bible (AMP) © 1965, 1987 by Zondervan Publishing House.

Printed in the United States of America

For information:
Multnomah Publishers, Inc. • P. O. Box 1720 • Sisters, OR 97759

Library of Congress Cataloging-in-Publication Data
Vredevelt, Pam W., 1955–
Espresso for a woman's spirit: encouraging stories of hope and humor / by Pam Vredevelt.
    p. cm.
Includes bibliographical references.
ISBN 1-57673-636-9
1. Christian women—Religious aspects—Anecdotes. 2. Christian women—Religious life—
Humor. 3. Christian women—Conduct of life—Humor. 4. Women—Spiritual healing. I. Title
BV4527.V74 2000
248.8'43—dc21
00-008959

00 01 02 03 04 05 06 07—10 9 8 7 6 5 4 3 2 1 0

*To my mom, Dana Walker,
and to my other dear friends who make me laugh
and remind me of my Source of hope
when I'm stretched to capacity
and plumb worn out.*

Contents

Contents

Acknowledgments

It's fun to visit new coffee shops and taste unique creations prepared to order. I love the times that I find a brew with just the right blend of ingredients to make an irresistible latte.

What first-class coffee shops do with coffee, Holly Halverson does with written text. She has taken my stories and added just the right ingredients to heighten poignancy and intensify impact. My deep gratitude to you, Holly, for investing your time and talent so that we can serve a delicious brew of hope and humor to women across the country. And Larry Libby, I've thanked the Lord for blessing me and the reader with the softening touches and sparkle you've added.

My thanks to the Multnomah family for encouraging me to write this series. Don and Brenda, you have helped me dream *big* again. Penny, your authenticity refreshes me. Ken, your direction has been keen and has delivered some surprise blessings. And to all the others in-house—your enthusiasm about *Espresso for Your Spirit* has energized me to keep the coffeepot on and the ideas flowing.

And my sincere thanks to Doug Benson for your computer savvy and tenacity in conducting thorough Internet searches for me. If there were a needle in a haystack, I have every confidence that you'd be the first one to find it!

INTRODUCTION

A First Sip

"So this is what they call writer's block," I said to my husband, John, as we were sitting in front of the fire one evening. Other than writing in my prayer journal during quiet times with the Lord, I had not touched a pen to paper for weeks. Even worse than my inability to translate thoughts to print, though, was my lack of inspiration. Frankly, I had nothing to say. I had never been at a loss for words before, so this was a bit baffling to both of us.

"I think you're just tired and need some time to recharge," John reassured me.

He was right. I had pushed hard to meet a deadline for my latest book, *Espresso for Your Spirit: Hope and Humor for Pooped Out Parents.* Since my creative juices flow best during the morning hours, fueled by a hot cup of fresh-brewed coffee, I'd been rising earlier and earlier to tackle my to-do list. Consequently my beauty sleep had been shaved to the bare minimum. A decrease in sleep, an increase in the kids' sports programs and homework, plus my usual household and job responsibilities added up to a draining equation. I felt like the life had been sucked right out of me.

Sound familiar?

I know I'm not alone. It seems as if everywhere I turn I hear women say, "I'm exhausted!" Whether they are wives, mothers, employees—or any combination of the three—the overriding theme I hear is one of being worn out. Many have become accustomed to running on fumes. They have mastered the art of depriving and neglecting their bodies, minds, and spirits. Exhaustion has become a way of life. Too many demands. Too many needs. Too many deadlines. Too little time. You know the story.

One of the things I say to the clients I counsel is: "Pam's prescription for fatigue is rest, time with the Lord, and a latte topped with whipped cream and chocolate sprinkles."

When I encountered my own bout of burnout in the form of writer's block, I took a healthy dose of my own medicine. For six consecutive months, I streamlined my activities and simplified my life by saying no to everything but the bare necessities. This freed up some time for me to devour several good books and to read the Scriptures. Each day I carved out space in my schedule to write in my prayer journal and reflect on things the Lord was saying to me.

Six months ago my cup was bone-dry.

Now it is overflowing.

Espresso for a Woman's Spirit: Encouraging Stories of Hope and Humor is the result.

I wrote this book especially for those of you who—like me—have found yourselves tuckered out. It is for women who need a few sacred moments of relief from the grueling grind of life…and some nourishment for your spirit.

I remember a verse I heard for the first time many years ago. God says, "Behold, I stand at the door [of your heart], and knock: if any man [or woman] hear my voice, and open the door, I will come in to him, and will sup with him, and he with me" (Revelation 3:20, KJV).

"Sup"? I wondered. *What's "sup"?* I'd never heard the word before. Come to find out, "sup" is an old King James word that simply means *share an evening meal together.* And what do you experience around the table? Companionship. Meaningful discussion. Being together.

Today, where does that soul-to-soul connection take place? Where do people like to meet together? In the Pacific Northwest, coffee shops are a favorite place to rendezvous. Those of us journeying through the second millennium often "sup" best while holding a warm cup of coffee.

It's easy for me to imagine God walking into a coffee shop, pulling up a chair, and joining a group of ladies holding lattes. Why? Because God longs for relationship with us. He wants to be our companion through life. He yearns to hear our thoughts and feelings and to share His perspectives with us. A coffee shop would be an easy place for Him to connect with those He loves.

I think sometimes we get things mixed up. We think God is more interested in our following rules and regulations than in our building a relationship with Him. In mandates rather than mentoring. In disciplines rather than discipleship. When we conclude this, we miss the essence of the main message of the Bible. Dos and don'ts will never change our lives. But an intimate relationship with the living God will.

It's my prayer that *Espresso for a Woman's Spirit* will prompt moments of deep communion with Him. When the Spirit of God knocks on the door of your heart, open it wide, and invite Him to join you for some sweet fellowship. First, brew a steaming cup of your favorite coffee. Then find a few cushy pillows in a quiet, cozy spot. Inwardly tune your ears to hear what God wants to say to you. Then come to these pages and banish fatigue with spiritual reflections, hope-filled stories, and chuckle-worthy anecdotes.

If you'd like an extra shot of spiritual stimulation, form a Koffee Klatch with a few friends, read *Espresso* together, and savor some heart-to-heart sharing using the questions in the back of the book. Great encouragement and healing can come when women bear one another's burdens.

I do hope each sip of a chapter leaves you feeling energized and craving more.

With a hug (and a latte) for your journey,

Pam Vredevelt

CHAPTER 1

A Reminder to Remember

I will remember the deeds of the LORD;
yes, I will remember your miracles of long ago.

Psalm 77:11

If you're reading this book, I have a strong hunch that now and then you may be a victim of the Worn-Out Woman Syndrome. Am I right? You've given all you have (and more) to the needy people and causes that fill your life. Consequently your last reserve of energy has circled—and descended—the drain. Yet you still want to contribute to the world around you: to meet your family's needs, fulfill the demands of your job, and bring all the vivacity and help you can to your ministry. So here you are, sitting (I hope) somewhere comfortable, savoring a steaming mug of fresh java, and reading these words hoping that this book will do for your soul what coffee does for the mind: warm, stimulate, inspire.

As I said in the introduction, I know exactly how you feel. And I've noticed something about myself—and, perhaps, women in general. When we are particularly tired or stressed, our thoughts can easily wander onto a negative track. Fatigue fuels faulty thinking and creates faith crises. It skews judgment and causes us to view life with a pessimistic twist.

On the other hand, rest, time with God, and—another tool I've used through the years—*the deliberate recall of His goodness* can lead us out of the gloomy swamps back onto a path that climbs toward the high country. Remembering is a good life strategy. It's what David did when he was worn so thin that he didn't know if he could face another day in this world.

David was a man with a big heart and a tall assignment who knew well the highest highs and deepest lows that come with life. In one psalm, his words reflect utter exhaustion:

> I cry to the Lord; I call and call to him. Oh, that he would listen. I am in deep trouble and I need his help so badly. All night long I pray, lifting my hands to heaven, pleading. There can be no joy for me until he acts. I think of God and moan, overwhelmed with longing for his help. I cannot sleep until you act. I am too distressed even to pray!
>
> Has the Lord rejected me forever? Will he never again be favorable? Is his lovingkindness gone forever?

Has his promise failed? Has he forgotten to be kind to one so undeserving? Has he slammed the door in anger on his love? And I said: This is my fate, that the blessings of God have changed to hate. (Psalm 77:1–4, 7–10, TLB)

You can see that David knew how we feel sometimes. But if you read on, you'll discover that David's mood and tone did an about-face. Suddenly a song of praise bubbled from the depths of his dark pool of despair: "O God, your ways are holy. Where is there any other as mighty as you? You are the God of miracles and wonders! You still demonstrate your awesome power" (Psalm 77:13–14, TLB).

What happened? What created the change in his heart? What washed away David's grief? The key is sandwiched between verses 10 and 13. The passage tells us that David paused and remembered. He recounted God's faithful acts of love from his past: "I recall the many miracles he did for me so long ago. Those wonderful deeds are constantly in my thoughts. I cannot stop thinking about them" (Psalm 77:11–12, TLB).

How about you? What do you do when you're so beaten down that you're too tired to pray? David revealed a great pattern to follow. He remembered. He listed all the times that God made a difference in his past.

All of us have pivotal experiences of God's loving activity in our

lives. We may not have recognized them at the time, but God has been actively involved in our lives from day one. Think about it.

- Have you ever had a narrow escape from a tough situation by some strange protection? Have you considered the possibility that God was the one who rescued you?
- Have you ever received a blessing that you know you didn't earn? God is the giver of all good gifts.
- Have you ever steered away from trouble and toward something more noble because something inside you quietly craved purity? Only God inspires a desire for holiness.
- Have you ever gone through a hard time only to discover later that it prepared you for something greater in your life? God is good at bringing value out of adversity.
- Have you ever made a good decision that took you in a surprisingly positive direction just because you felt impressed to do so? My hunch is, God was speaking to you.[1]

Some of us probably have had moments like these and just discounted them as coincidence, fluke, or "dumb luck." Or we may have celebrated some of these divine interventions at the time but then lost sight of them in the fog of daily life. The question really is not whether we have had moments when God intervened in our lives. The question is: What have we done with them?[2]

Not long ago I had occasion to harness the faith-building

power of remembering God's interventions in my past. John and I were sitting in the front row of an auditorium, waiting for our cue to step up on the platform. We were team-teaching a group of about five thousand people that weekend. As I looked over the sea of faces to my left and right, my stomach started doing flip-flops and I found myself thinking, *What in the world am I doing here? I'm a therapist. I'm a trained listener. I have big ears! John's the one in our family with the big...well,* he's *the preacher.*

But then I remembered. I recalled a fateful day in 1975 when I heard nationally known author Joyce Landorf—and God—speak. I will tell the story more fully in chapter 4, but for now just let me say that God told me, in unmistakable terms, that I would one day do exactly what Joyce Landorf was doing. When I faced the audience I was supposed to teach—a fulfillment of God's word to me—I reminisced for a moment about the clarity of God's call that day and the way He had unfolded His plan since. I remembered that He had led me to use my knowledge and experience to help others as a counselor, and I realized that teaching and public speaking were simply a natural extension of that assignment.

I calmed down. God had called me, so God would empower me. That's how He works.

Remembering God's interventions in my past gives me the faith and courage to face the tasks that are in front of me now.

How easy it is to forget. The memory dulls. We start to

retrieve something from our mental files, and the cabinet locks up on us. But it's worth the effort. Remembering how God has intercepted us in the past can increase our faith today and empower us to tackle whatever challenges confront us. And if we are ever going to get past the Worn-Out Woman Syndrome, we have to learn to use this powerful tool.

For years I've applied the technique of recalling positive memories to empower my clients to perform at their peak. I've worked with a number of top collegiate athletes. Before a race or a game, they needed to mentally prepare themselves. I told them they had a choice. They could rehearse the occasions in their pasts when they had made mistakes and fallen apart under the pressure, or they could recall the times they had played at peak performance. Which memories do you think spurred them toward success? Memories can beef up our courage.

If recalling positive memories can enhance an athlete's performance, imagine the difference it can make in building our faith and refreshing our spirit for managing the pressures of every day. Imagine the power it can have in healing the bitterness attached to any bad memories we have nursed in our imaginations. A friend of mine was able to conquer resentment toward her father by spending less and less time thinking about the bad memories she had cherished for many years and concentrating on the good ones that remained.

In some ways I think our spiritual lives become dwarfed

when we forget our pasts. There is a propensity in our high-pressured, fast-paced society to allow the urgent demands of today and the worries of tomorrow to dominate our thinking. We live in the information age, and it's easy to jump to the conclusion that if we just gather new facts, secure more data, or run tighter calculations, our problems will be solved. It seems to me that there are times when seeking more information or advice is not the prescription of choice—but remembering is.

Seven years ago, when our son Nathan was born with Down's syndrome, John and I went through a deep grieving process. We gathered information about the diagnosis, read book after book, and talked with specialists. We wanted to understand his condition to the best of our ability. But do you know what? Stockpiling all that information didn't do anything to ease our pain. In fact, there were times when we didn't want to read or hear or absorb *one more thing* about Down's syndrome. Why? Because the very same information that increased our awareness also fed our fears.

The reality was that when we considered the future of raising a mentally retarded son, we needed more than information. We needed some real-life, rock-solid reminders that God had not abandoned us. We needed some tangible reasons for our hope. That's what remembering does for us.

Doesn't it make sense to build your faith on what you *do* know rather than on what you don't? I don't know why Nathan was born with Down's syndrome. I don't know why he hasn't been able to learn to talk. I don't know whether or not he will ever have the capacity to live and work on his own. Only time will tell. And I could spend a lot of time focusing on all I don't know and watch my faith erode. Or I can spend my time rehearsing what I know for sure, which is what David said: "You are the God of miracles and wonders! You still demonstrate your awesome power."

How about you? What truths do your stories tell? When did God intervene in your past and help you in ways that defied human reason? Why not take a few moments in the presence of the omniscient One to recall your own divine appointments? If you need help, just ask. The Lord can open your eyes and enlarge your perspective.

Jesus said, "The Counselor, the Holy Spirit, whom the Father will send in my name, will teach you all things and will *remind* you of everything I have said to you" (John 14:26, NIV; emphasis mine). Why? Because when you need encouragement, remembering matters.

Recalling empowers.

Reflecting energizes.

Reminiscing refills our cup.

Power Perks: A Sip of Hope and Humor

Three elderly ladies were discussing the travails of getting older. One said, "Sometimes I catch myself with a jar of mayonnaise in my hand in front of the refrigerator and can't remember whether I need to put it away, or start making a sandwich."

The second lady chimed in, "Yes, sometimes I find myself on the landing of the stairs and can't remember whether I was on my way up or on my way down."

The third one responded, "Well, I'm glad I don't have that problem; knock on wood." As she rapped her knuckles on the table, she said, "That must be the door, I'll get it!"

"It is a delightful and profitable occupation to mark the hand of God in the lives of ancient saints, and to observe His goodness in delivering them, His mercy in pardoning them, and His faithfulness in keeping His covenant with them. But would it not be even more interesting and profitable for us to mark the hand of God in our own lives? Ought we not to look upon our own history as being at least as full of God, as full of His goodness and of His truth, as much a proof of His faithfulness and veracity, and the lives of those who have gone before? Let us review our own lives. Surely in these memories we will discover incidents refreshing to ourselves and glorifying to our God."

—Charles Spurgeon[3]

"Each man's memory is his private literature."

—Aldous Huxley[4]

"Do not forget the things I have done throughout history. For I am God—I alone!…Only I can tell you what is going to happen even before it happens. Everything I plan will come to pass."

—Isaiah 46:9–10, NLT

CHAPTER 2
Solitary Springs

*Come to me with your ears wide open.
Listen, for the life of your soul is at stake.*

Isaiah 55:3, TLB

"Pam, you have an emergency phone call. Nathan left the schoolyard. They have searched for the last half hour and can't find him, so they are calling the police." My secretary's face showed alarm as she stood in my office doorway.

That news would send icy shivers through any mother, but my fear escalated in light of Nathan's Down's syndrome. His wandering lacks the safety valves of common sense and maturity. Outside of adult supervision, Nathan's risk of encountering danger increases exponentially.

Adrenaline coursed through my veins as I rushed to the

phone my secretary held for me. "Hello, this is Pam," I said, trying to maintain my cool.

Nathan's teacher said, "Pam, somehow Nathan left the school grounds during recess, and we have looked everywhere. The principal is searching the surrounding neighborhoods. Our aids are combing the schoolyard and adjacent properties. We're going to call the police in to help."

"I'm on my way."

By the time I reached my car, my stomach was tied up in knots. A lump the size of a Ping-Pong ball seemed wedged against my larynx. It's amazing what anxiety does to the body. I began playing therapist with myself.

Okay, Pam. Calm down. God knows right where Nathan is. There are a lot of people looking for him. Keep your cool. Don't jump to conclusions. You won't be any help to anybody if you start short-circuiting. Just relax. You'll be at the school in five minutes.

That was the plan.

But you know how plans go.

When I started the car, a buzzer signaled that my gas tank was empty. I had intended to get gas on the way to work that morning, but I was running late. I figured I could make it to the office and fill the tank after work.

Now, what do you think a professional therapist would do in a situation like this? Would she respond with logic and say, "Hmm. It looks like I need gas"? Would she maintain complete composure, casually shrug, and say, "Oh well, what's another kink in the day?" Or would she flail her hands, scream *"Oh no!"* at the gas gauge, and then burst into tears?

Yup, you guessed it. Obviously my car wasn't the only thing running on fumes at the moment. After my little fit, I pulled it together long enough to pray, *God, please get me to the gas station that's on the way to the school.*

He did. But I should have prayed for the people at the station because they were slower than slugs on a Portland sidewalk. For several l-o-n-g minutes, I was the only car at the pumps, and no one responded. If the Lord was testing my patience, I flunked. After waiting, and waiting, I finally went into the station and said, "Could someone please help me? I'm in a hurry. My little boy is lost, and I need to go find him."

The guy dawdling behind the counter acted like he didn't have a care in the world. He cocked his head to the side, squinted his eyes, and gave me the look. You know—the one that says, "Yeah, sure, lady." He s-l-o-w-l-y made his way to the pumps. Twelve and a half minutes later, I rolled out of the station with enough repressed negative energy in my body to trigger a turn-of-the-century eruption on Mount Saint Helens. You want to see fireworks? I could have shot off a display more spectacular than the New Year's Eve show on the Eiffel Tower.

Panic-driven thoughts ricocheted in my brain. *What if we can't find Nathan? What if he wanders onto a busy street? What if a crook gets hold of him?* Pictures on milk cartons flashed before my eyes. A vivid imagination is a blessing for creative writing, but it's a curse in these kinds of situations.

I finally arrived at the school. Racing up to the front doors, I passed a woman walking toward the parking lot. I must have had *panicked mother* written all over my face because she looked at me and asked, "Are you Nathan's mom?"

"Yes," I replied anxiously, hoping she had some good news for me.

"They found Nathan."

"Oh, thank God," I said.

"He's in with the principal," she added.

Sure enough. There was my guilty little escapee sitting in the principal's office with a very somber look on his face. I can't remember an occasion when Nathan didn't smile and jump up to give me a welcome hug after we'd been apart for a few hours. But this time he didn't move. His head hung low, and he looked at me through guilty eyes, knowing he had made a *big* boo-boo.

As I hugged him I said gently, "Nathan, I was scared and very worried about you. And the principal and your teachers were very concerned, too. Leaving the schoolyard was not a good idea."

The principal gave me the full story. Somehow Nathan had sneaked around back of the school, pushed the gate open, and wandered over to a retirement home next door. He apparently

had gone to the third floor of the complex (Nathan loves eleva-
tors and is proficient at working them), roamed the halls, and
then went back down to ground level and out the back door. I
guess he'd seen enough of the old folks and decided it was time
for something a bit more exciting.

Driven by his unquenchable thirst for adventure, he bolted
over to the next building on the block, which happened to be a
hospital. That's where a kind elderly man noticed that Nathan
was handicapped and all alone in the hospital lobby. Figuring
Nathan was lost, he took him by the hand and began hunting. A
member of the school search party rounded the corner a few
minutes later.

Nathan spent the rest of the afternoon in the principal's
office with the school counselor. She drew pictures of the event
to help him clearly understand what choices were acceptable and
what choices were not. I am so thankful for these added sources
of support as we try to help Nathan grow up to be safe and wise.

I think I pumped more adrenaline during that episode than
I had during the entire previous month. And boy oh boy did my
body feel it the next day. When the alarm went off at 5:30 A.M. I
felt like I'd been hit by a Mack truck. The impact wasn't just
physical. My mind was troubled, and anxiety had me around the
throat. My frustration about the day before was matched only by
my apprehension of what was to come.

Ever experience that? Ever have a day so full of panic that

even when the situation is resolved, fear's residue remains and taints your outlook? That's when we need some time with God the most—when He has just recently seemed far away.

I forced myself out of bed, knowing I needed God to speak to me. I needed solitude. I needed quiet. And I needed the words of the Spirit to breathe life into my worn-out soul.

The morning following Nathan's escape, I made myself a cup of coffee, found a comfortable seat in the living room, and dialed God's home number. It was a short prayer. Nothing complicated— simply a soul's cry for help: *Lord, You know how troubled I am about Nathan. I need You to speak to me today. Please give me Your perspective and help me hear what You want to say to me this morning.*

For the last two years I had been reading each morning from the *Change Your Life Daily Bible.* Each calendar day of the year lists passages of Scripture to read from the Old and New Testaments. As I read the passages for that day, I jotted down a few verses.

I will make springs in the desert, so that my chosen people can be refreshed. (Isaiah 43:20, NLT)

I will give you abundant water to quench your thirst and to moisten your parched fields. And I will pour out my Spirit and my blessings on your children. They will thrive like watered grass, like willows on a riverbank. (Isaiah 44:3–4, NLT)

And I will give you treasures hidden in the darkness—
secret riches. I will do this so you may know that I am
the LORD, the God of Israel, the one who calls you by
name. (Isaiah 45:3, NLT)

Now glory be to God! By his mighty power at work
within us, he is able to accomplish infinitely more than
we would ever dare to ask or hope. (Ephesians 3:20, NLT)

The sequence and content of the verses rang with meaning.
I recorded in my journal what the Lord seemed to be saying to
me: "Pam, when life escorts you into a hot, dry, barren desert,
look to Me. I always have what you need. I will refresh you. You
can never deplete My abundant supply. I have enough—and
more than enough—for you and your children. I will pour out
My Spirit and bless your children today. They will thrive. And in
the middle of the hardships and the dark times you endure, I will
give you treasures—treasures that can be found only in the
dark—that prove My love and that I am intimately aware of
everything going on in your life. I understand your weaknesses
and vulnerabilities. But don't be fooled by your feelings. My
Spirit lives in you, and He is able to accomplish more than you
have ever imagined. So rest. Trust. Let My words empower you.
They are spirit, and they are your very life."

I closed my Bible that morning with a much healthier outlook on the day. My body still felt bulldozed, but my mind was

more settled. Even though nothing had really changed on the outside, I was different on the inside. Out of a chaotic mishmash of emotion had come order and focus. A spirit of faith had pulled rank on my fears.

That's the power of a little bit of solitude coupled with an open heart to God. It seems to me that there are certain springs that can be tapped only when we are still in God's presence. Quietness activates my mind. It gives me a chance to attend to what is going on inside my soul and to hear what God has to say to me. "Be still, and know that I am God," the psalmist says.

Perhaps stillness is a prerequisite for knowing.

That's why I make it a specific daily goal to be alone for a while. It allows me to calm down. I take some time away from the noise, the appointments, the projects. I put aside the endless distractions, the compulsive duties, the unnecessary errands. Unchecked, my responsibilities can drain my cup dry. I must make room in my schedule to replenish my spirit if I'm going to be the woman I really want to be.

It seems to me that we, as modern-day American women, should have an edge over previous generations in working periods of solitude into our schedule. We have a plethora of convenience items to reduce our time commitments on every conceivable task. A dishwasher scrubs our plates. A washer cleans and a dryer fluffs our clothes. Cars and planes provide speedy travel. Electric dust-devourers clear the rubble from our floors. Fiber optics perfect our long-distance communication. The Internet puts a wealth of information at our fingertips. The microwave serves dinner in three minutes. And fast-food restaurants cook for us when we don't have time to get home between activities.

Functionally we have gained.

But spiritually—I'm not so sure.

With all of our free time, it seems we are still prone to draining our energy reserves rather than replenishing them. It's easy to throw ourselves into all kinds of causes involving our spouses, our children, our professions, and our ministries without evaluating the cost.

While many of these commitments are noble, I often have to stop and ask myself if they are right for me at this particular time in my life. Is an invitation to sit on a board of directors something God wants me to do with my time—today, now? If I say yes to one request, what will I need to say no to in order to keep balance? To throw myself indiscriminately into activities without hearing from God will accomplish little beyond creating an anemic spirit and a fragmented sense of well-being.

I've seen a pattern in the counseling office. The more pulled apart and conflicted a woman feels, the more driven she is to try to quiet her turmoil by adding more diversions and unceasing activity to her plate. Rollo Mays said it well: "It's an old and ironic habit of the human race to run faster when we have lost our way."

But chasing after seducing externals does not have the power to fill our internal void. Throwing ourselves into random activity to drown out the cries of the soul won't work. It's about as effective as a mother hoping to quiet a crying baby by scrubbing the kitchen floor. The only way to still a hungry baby is to offer it the breast or warm a bottle of milk and feed it. Likewise, the only way to quiet a thirsty, conflicted soul is to pay attention to its cries and respond with the appropriate nourishment. Jesus said, "Whoever drinks the water I give him will never thirst. Indeed, the water I give him will become in him a spring of water welling up to eternal life" (John 4:14).

For me it's during the early morning, when the noises on the outside are muted, that I'm better able to hear the needs within. For others it's in the afternoon when the children are napping, or in the evening before they turn out the lights. The time of day we meet with God is irrelevant. Regardless of when you package them into your day, there is strength found in still moments with God. Isn't that what Isaiah meant when he wrote, "In quietness and trust is your strength" (Isaiah 30:15)?

Running on empty, in cars or in life, isn't anyone's cup of espresso. If we take time instead to regularly drink words of spirit and life, we can face the day's demands—including emergency phone calls—with courage, energy, and wisdom.

Jesus' springs overflow with them.

Drink with me.

Power Perks: A Sip of Hope and Humor

A young woman walked into a bank in New York City and asked for the loan officer. She said that she was going to Europe on business for two weeks and needed to borrow five thousand dollars. The bank officer said that the bank needed some kind of security for such a loan, so the woman handed him the keys to a new Rolls Royce parked on the street in front of the bank. Everything checked out, and the bank agreed to accept the car as collateral for the loan. An employee drove the Rolls into the bank's garage and parked it.

Two weeks later, the woman returned, paid the five thousand dollars and the interest, which came to $15.41. The loan officer said, "Ma'am, we are happy to have had your business, and this transaction has worked out very nicely. But we are a little puzzled. While you were away, we conducted a more thorough background check and found that you are a multimillionaire. We were wondering why you would bother to borrow five thousand dollars."

The woman replied, "Where else in New York can I park my car for two weeks for fifteen bucks?"

Call it Java, bean drink, roasted-black water, the writer's drug, steamin' tar, roasted caffeine or coffee, just make sure it's in a cup near my bed when I awake.

Nelson Lin[1]

Half an hour's listening is essential except when you are very busy. Then a full hour is needed.[2]

I cannot be the woman I should be without times of quietness. Stillness is an essential part of growing deeper.[3]

CHAPTER 3

The Gift of Faith

*L**et love be your greatest aim; nevertheless,*
ask also for the special abilities the Holy Spirit gives.

1 Corinthians 14:1, TLB

Funny thing—the week or two after Nathan wandered off the school grounds, I was jumpy. Every time the phone rang I got a knot in my stomach, wondering if it was the school again. I kept fearing I would hear, "Mrs. Vredevelt, it's your son. We've called in the police to help...." The stress of the previous week had shaken me, and my defenses were still a bit weak.

Despite the spiritual homework I had done the day after Nathan's escape, what I faced in the days that followed was normal. It's not unusual to struggle with a heightened sense of apprehension following a crisis, an unexpected hardship, or a major change.

It takes time and energy for the mind and body to adjust and settle down. Replenishment is never a "done deal," but something we have to continually practice to ward off fresh stabs of anxiety.

Some who weather severe crises or multiple chronic stresses become hypervigilant, looking for danger lurking around every turn. I recently spoke at a women's retreat, where around the dinner table I heard ladies making these comments: "I'm in a really good place right now, but I keep wondering when the other shoe is going to drop."

"My kids are having a great year—knock on wood—but I don't know how long that's going to last."

"Things are going well. But I'm afraid to be too happy because I don't want to be disappointed again."

Anxiety had crept in, taken hold, and was blocking these ladies from enjoying the good times afforded them. Ever been there—stuck? Ever struggled with a gnawing sense of anxiety about what's around the corner?

One of my specialties as a therapist is working with posttraumatic stress victims. I know the symptoms inside and out. During the years following Nathan's entry into this world—six weeks early, with severe heart complications, and a surprise diagnosis of Down's syndrome—it was hard for me to admit that I struggled with some of them myself. On the heels of that crisis I experienced a floating foreboding, a nagging suspicion that something bad was going to happen. I carried irrational fears that

John or our other children, Jessie and Ben, would be harmed, or worse yet, die.

I used all the therapeutic interventions I knew to combat the unwelcome anxiety. Healthy self-talk, prayer, Scripture, praise songs, diversions, debriefing with friends, exercise—you name it; I did it. And much of the time I found relief. But a turning point came for me one morning when I was reading through Paul's letter to the Corinthians. It was a passage I had read many times before, but on that particular morning it carried a new meaning for me.

> Now there are different kinds of spiritual gifts, but it is the same Holy Spirit who is the source of them all.... A spiritual gift is given to each of us as a means of helping the entire church.
>
> To one person the Spirit gives the ability to give wise advice; to another he gives the gift of special knowledge. The Spirit gives special faith to another, and to someone else he gives the power to heal the sick.... It is the one and only Holy Spirit who distributes these gifts. (1 Corinthians 12:4, 7–9, 11, NLT)

As I reflected on these verses, I knew I had a measure of faith. But they talked about a special gift of faith imparted by the Spirit of God that goes beyond the norm. In this context, it's a faith that enables a person to be fully persuaded by and completely reliant on the truthfulness of God.

I want this, Lord! I exclaimed to myself. *Unnecessary fears are getting the best of me. I need a spirit of faith. It says here that You give special faith to some—I want all You have to give, Lord.*

I can't tell you that all my fears dissolved with that thirty-second prayer, but I can tell you that I began to sense a greater propensity in my spirit to believe God for whatever I needed at any given time. As I continued to replenish my spirit and open my heart to the Lord, fear became more manageable.

In the process, it became ever so clear to me that faith and fear are powerful opposites. Faith doesn't necessarily make all of our fears disappear. We live in an unpredictable and inconsistent world that evokes anxiety. We live with the accuser of the brethren, who taunts us with a spirit of fear. But faith empowers us to be women of courage who can cope with life's hardships.

Years ago I saw a clever acrostic for the word *fear: F*alse *E*vidence *A*ppearing *R*eal. When we are fearful, we tend to jump to negative conclusions that are based on partial truth, not complete and accurate evidence. When something goes wrong, like greased lightning we forecast the worst-case scenario.

Again, after a trauma, it's a natural response, but a troublesome one. In such times, we need truth. Seven years ago, after Nathan's earthshattering entrance into the world, I developed an acrostic for the word *faith* to use when I was caught in the crossfire of scary thoughts: *F*ully *A*bandoned (to God) *I*n *T*rust (and) *H*umility.

When I'm facing trials and tribulations, when I'm vulnerable to those gnawing "what ifs," I need to activate my faith. I need to tilt my head heavenward, raise my hands in surrender, and say, "God, no matter what, I am fully abandoned to You in trust and humility." It was a posture I sensed in a man whose faith caused Jesus to marvel. His story unfolds in Matthew:

> When Jesus entered Capernaum, a centurion came to him, asking for help. "Lord," he said, "my servant lies at home paralyzed and in terrible suffering."
>
> Jesus said to him, "I will go and heal him."
>
> The centurion replied, "Lord, I do not deserve to have you come under my roof. But just say the word, and my servant will be healed. For I myself am a man under authority, with soldiers under me. I tell this one, 'Go,' and he goes; and that one, 'Come,' and he comes. I say to my servant, 'Do this,' and he does it."
>
> When Jesus heard this, he *was astonished* and said to those following him, "I tell you the truth, I have not found anyone in Israel with such great faith...."
>
> Then Jesus said to the centurion, "Go! It will be done just as you believed it would." And his servant was healed at that very hour. (Matthew 8:5–10, 13, emphasis mine)

I read this story through several times and wondered what Jesus saw in this man's heart. He wasn't a religious leader. He wasn't even a Jew. He was a Roman soldier. Think about it: For years Jesus had mixed with the most religious people of His day. He had rubbed shoulders with prominent Old Testament scholars. He had personally trained and mentored a select few. But He said that in all of His lifetime, He had not met anyone who had responded in such a way.

I searched the story to find out why the man had received such an accolade. He doesn't appear to have done anything. Jesus' disciples had been performing mind-boggling miracles among the crowds, yet the Lord didn't single out any of them as having tremendous faith. What did Jesus see in this soldier?

The first, most obvious answer, of course, is the sheer strength of the man's faith. Here was a Gentile who immediately recognized what the majority of Jews failed to even glimpse: the power and authority of God's Son. The story says this Roman officer called him "Lord." That may not seem like a big deal to you, but back then it was politically incorrect and a full-fledged no-no!

Understanding the historical context is critical. We know from numerous records that at the time all Roman citizens were required to reverence the emperor as their lord. Anything to the contrary would elicit severe punishment. This Roman soldier was well aware of the laws of the day. After all, he was one of the honored few who had earned the right to help the emperor enforce them. He knew when he publicly addressed Jesus as "Lord" that he was risking his life. Such an infraction was punishable at least by a loss in rank and at most by execution.

This man had power. He had wealth. He had trained and diligently worked for years to attain his status. Yet with a few public words about Jesus, he laid himself open to lose everything, including his life. The soldier's comment demonstrated total abandonment, complete trust, and absolute humility before the One whom he addressed as "Lord."[1]

Scores of people stood around Jesus and the soldier that day. Many believed Jesus could work miracles. But those seeking merely the miraculous didn't impress the Savior. Instead, He marveled at a man who, through enormous faith, was willing to entrust his total well-being to Him.

Do you know that there are only two places in Scripture where Jesus was amazed at anything? One is in this text. The other is where Jesus marveled at the unbelief exhibited by those in his hometown.

What the story of the Roman soldier says to me is that God doesn't want first place in my life. He wants all of my life. He wants me to totally abandon myself to Him. He wants me to entrust my well-being into His hands and to confidently believe in His ability to care for me.

Let's leave Capernaum and return to the harsh realities of where we live. When we are suffering hardship or emerging from the shadows of a dark time in our lives, our confidence is shaken.

Trauma breaks down our defenses and often creates a faith crisis. After a trauma we find ourselves asking questions that would be unthinkable in smoother days:

Where is God?

Does God love me?

Is God really in control?

How can anything good possibly come out of something so bad?

Grief distorts our perception. Pain requires a tremendous amount of emotional energy. There is little left over for anything other than mere survival.

If you have recently suffered a crisis, trauma, or major loss, please give yourself grace. Give yourself time to process the pain. And give God time to restore your bearings.

I was wobbly for a while after Nathan wandered from his school. But over time my anxieties largely subsided. I still frequently ask God to gift me with a spirit of faith that will enable me to fully abandon myself to Him in trust and humility. I am finding the practice of surrender to His ways and purposes becoming more habitual. When fear raises its ugly head, prompting me to forecast negatively, I am more proficient in making faith statements.

Remember, the battle of faith against fear is waged in the mind.

When you're in the middle of adversity:

Fear says, "God has left you. He doesn't care. You're on your own."

Faith says, "In God's kingdom everything is based on promise, not on feeling. God has a plan, and it is built on love."

When you've been ripped off by someone:

Fear says, "You can't trust people."

Faith says, "God, the Redeemer, restores stolen goods to their rightful owners, one way or another."

When you're the subject of slander:

Fear says, "Everyone is talking. Your reputation is smeared for life."

Faith says, "God will straighten the record when false things have been said about me."

When you've made a major blunder:

Fear says, "It's over. You've blown it. You may as well throw in the towel."

Faith says, "Failure is always an event, never a person. God will use my strengths and my weaknesses to accomplish His plans."

When you're waiting for something:

Fear says, "You're going to be on hold forever."

Faith says, "My time is in God's hands. His plans for me will be accomplished right on schedule."

When God says no to your prayers:

Fear says, "If God really loved you, He would give you what you want."

Faith says, "God is acting for my highest good."

When you experience failure:

Fear says, "You can't trust God. Look at how He's let you down."

Faith says, "God has proven His trustworthiness by dying for me."

When you're staggering under a load of guilt:

Fear says, "Your mistakes will haunt you the rest of your life."

Faith says, "God holds nothing against me. He has sovereignly declared me pardoned."

When you face stinging regret:

Fear says, "Your scars limit you."

Faith says, "I am useful to God not in spite of my scars, but because of them."

When a close friend has let you down:

Fear says, "Why bother? It's not worth going on."

Faith says, "God will take the bad choices others have made against me and use them for my ultimate good."

When you experience the pruning of God's sharp shears:

Fear says, "If God loved you, He wouldn't let you suffer like this."

Faith says, "God knows better than I what I need. Even Christ learned obedience through what He suffered."[2]

Friend, do our doubts and fears intimidate God? No. Do our feelings influence God's responses? No.

But our faith does.

Let's allow our anxieties to be a reminder of our need to do spiritual maintenance, to be fully abandoned to God in trust and humility. Let's use our fears to trigger a prayer:

> *God, please birth the gift of faith in my spirit today.*
> *Help me believe in ways I have not yet believed.*
> *Exchange a spirit of fear for a spirit of faith.*
> *Open the eyes of my heart to see the differences*
> *the gifts of Your Spirit are making in my life—today.*

On the heels of that kind of prayer, I think we may indeed give the Lord some more opportunities to marvel.

Power Perks: A Sip of Hope and Humor

Mom and Dad were watching TV when Mom said, "I'm tired, and it's getting late. I think I'll go to bed."

She went to the kitchen to make sandwiches for the next day's lunches, rinsed out the popcorn bowls, took meat out of the freezer for tomorrow's supper, checked the levels of the cereal boxes, filled the sugar container, put spoons and bowls on the table, and set the coffeepot for brewing the next morning.

She then transferred some wet clothes from washer to dryer, put a load of clothes into the wash, ironed a shirt, and secured a loose button.

She picked up the newspapers strewn on the floor, gathered the game pieces left on the table, and put the telephone book back into the drawer.

She watered the plants, emptied a wastebasket, and hung up a towel to dry.

She yawned and stretched and headed for the bedroom. She stopped by the desk and wrote a note to the teacher, counted out some cash for the field trip, and pulled a textbook out from hiding under the chair. She signed a birthday card for a friend, addressed and stamped the envelope, and wrote a quick list for the grocery store. She put both near her purse.

Mom then creamed her face, put on moisturizer, brushed and flossed her teeth, and trimmed her nails.

Hubby called, "I thought you were going to bed."

"I'm on my way, " she said.

She put some water into the dog's dish and let the cat out, then made sure the doors were locked. She looked in on each of the kids and turned out a bedside lamp, hung up a shirt, threw some dirty socks in the hamper, and had a brief conversation with the one still up doing homework.

Once in her own room, she set the alarm, laid out clothing for the next day, and straightened up the shoe rack. She added three things to her list of things to do for tomorrow.

About that time, the hubby turned off the TV and announced to no one in particular, "I'm going to bed." And he did.

A faith that hasn't been tested can't be trusted.

Adriane Rogers[3]

Doubt is not the opposite of faith; it is one element of faith.

Paul Tillich[4]

Faith is not shelter against difficulties, but belief in the face of all contradictions.

Paul Tournier[5]

CHAPTER 4

Seasons of Change

*A*man's steps are directed by the LORD.

Proverbs 20:24

Do you like to reminisce? I do. I visit my photo albums frequently. It helps me keep things in perspective, particularly when I'm weathering a turbulent period of life. As I look back on the last forty-plus years, memories of the various seasons of my life evoke an array of emotions. Some seasons have been exciting, exhilarating, and full of promise and energy. Others have been strength sapping, heart wrenching, and filled with grief.

But there is one thread of truth that I can see clearly woven through each and every season: God has a plan, and it is good.

I recently did something fun. I drew a timeline of my life to date and highlighted the major seasons of change along the journey. It was a great little exercise that produced insight. Suddenly

I was able to grasp a more global perspective of God's specific guidance in my life.

I started with the point in time when I invited God to be in the driver's seat of my life. That season of rebirth I call *Spring.* *Summer,* a period of fruitfulness, follows. Then a painful pruning period ushers in *Fall,* followed by long, difficult days that bring the feeling of *Winter.* But then, rest assured, *Spring* always returns.

The first Spring of my life occurred when I was a student at Upper Arlington High School in Columbus, Ohio. My friend Donna invited me to a Bible study where I heard for the first time that I could have a personal relationship with God. All I needed to do was open my heart, pray, and surrender my life to Him. I did so, and that evening the Spirit of God created new life in my spirit and a hunger to know God like never before.

Summer arrived months later when, through a series of incredible events, my entire family, including grandparents, aunts, uncles, and cousins, came to know the Lord. The subsequent high school years were fun and fruitful. I had wonderful friends and was involved in dance team, clubs, and Bible study. To my astonishment, I was voted homecoming queen. But soon after all the festivities came news from my father that led to a season of Fall.

My dad was offered a new and exciting job opportunity in California. I was glad for my dad but sad for me. I wasn't ready to make such a drastic change. In January of my senior year, my family moved to California. I stayed in Ohio and lived with my grandparents so I could graduate with my class. Separation from my family was painful.

Winter arrived two days after graduation. I said good-bye to my grandparents and friends and moved to California. I felt like I was starting life over from scratch. How does a seventeen-year-old girl make friends in a new town without school as a gathering place? I took a job as a lifeguard, thinking I might meet some people, but the other guards at the pool were close friends and apparently not interested in widening the circle. Then the guy I had been dating in Ohio decided it was time to move on. Though it was summer outside, it was cold and lonely Winter in my soul.

But God had a plan, and it was good.

Sometime during that frosty season, the back burner on our stove went out. Mom called a repairman, and while he was fixing the burner, he told us of a contractor who could construct a retaining wall along the side of our property lined by a creek. The contractor's name was Ben Vredevelt.

Ben came to the house, bid on the job, and invited our family to visit Los Gatos Christian Church the following Sunday. I'll never forget that day. We walked into the back of the building, and the place was packed. On the platform stood one hundred college-age young adults ready to perform a musical.

The music started, and the lead singer stepped up to the microphone. He sang a song that moved me to tears. His countenance was radiant and, wow, was he handsome. There was something about his experience with God that seemed beyond what I had ever known. Yet I found him intriguing, even from a distance.

I found out later that his name was John Vredevelt. I learned that he and the homecoming queen from some school in the area had been an "item" for more than a year. I figured he was out of my league anyway.

By 1974 Spring had returned. I was enjoying many wonderful friendships with college students from the church. During those exciting months, a hunger to understand the Scriptures grew so strong within me that I chose not to complete my plans to attend Auburn University in Alabama. Instead I set my sails for Multnomah School of the Bible in Portland. There were nine young adults from the college group who enrolled at Multnomah that year. One of them just happened to be the talented and handsome John Vredevelt.

Believe me, Spring was in the air!

John and I became good friends that year. I happened to date his roommate, and he happened to date my roommate, and they happened to be brother and sister. The four of us had great fun together. But as young loves go, Nancy broke up with John, and Craig broke up with me, and John and I moaned and groaned together. Our bleeding hearts bonded, and we became the best of pals as well as singing partners. He and I and a friend formed His Life Trio, cut a record, and represented our school in concerts up and down the West Coast.

Over the next year our friendship blossomed into romantic love, and in 1975 John asked me to marry him. I thought about it, prayed all of three seconds, and blurted out a very enthusiastic, "Yes!"

Summer arrived in 1976. The warm sun, blue sky, and rolling green foothills of Los Gatos, California, set the stage for a beautiful ceremony as John and I said our wedding vows. One week later we packed our things and headed back to Oregon to complete our senior year of college. An elderly man with a great big heart and home rented us our first apartment for ninety dollars a month. The place was completely furnished, and the owner paid all the utilities. It was quite a deal for two poor, full-time students!

September 7, 1976—one month from the day of our wedding—ushered in Fall and Winter. We received the difficult news that John's dad had died suddenly of a heart attack. We descended instantly from the high of our honeymoon and discovered ourselves in a place neither of us had been before: deep grief.

Yet God had a plan, and it was good.

During this season a significant incident occurred. One weekend some friends invited John and me to attend an outdoor festival in Salem. Top-notch communicators and musicians from across the country gathered for a week of inspirational concerts and teaching. I was sitting in the back of a huge tented auditorium, listening to a woman on the platform talk about the difference God can make in our lives. I was engulfed in her stories, laughing with the others around me, when these words passed through my mind: *You'll be doing this someday.*

I thought it strange at the time because the woman on the platform was the noted author and national speaker Joyce Landorf. I had no aspirations to be a public speaker or to write a book. Though puzzled, I filed those words away in my heart.

Spring and Summer returned in 1978. John was hired as the youth pastor at East Hill Church in Gresham, Oregon, and I was on board as his assistant. We ate, drank, and slept youth ministry with three hundred lively and earnest kids. We had the time of our lives with them and couldn't have been more fulfilled.

Eventually, though, we endured some more Fall breezes. The church went through some major transitions, and one afternoon John came home and told me, "You no longer have a job." Finances were such that many staff members had been laid off. The news came as a shock and carried a sting. It was the first time in my life I had ever been "let go" from anything.

A few months later the Lord led me back to graduate school to study communications. It was a bittersweet season. I had been used to spending most of my time interacting with young people and partnering with John. Graduate school forced me into many long hours of solitude with my nose in books.

In 1986 I received a master's degree in communications. But that paled in comparison to the exciting news we heard a few months later. I was pregnant! After ten years of marriage, we were more than ready. But Spring never had a chance to come.

Winter arrived a brief five months later, when we learned that our baby had died in the womb. After a day of labor the baby was born, and we left the hospital with empty arms. Those were dark, cold days, filled with grief.

But God had a plan, and it was good.

I didn't realize exactly why God had led me to pursue a degree in communications. I simply found the subject fascinating, and I thought it might give me more tools for working with youth and small groups. But one afternoon a bigger picture began to come into focus. It was a few weeks after I delivered our stillborn baby, and I was at an athletic club, crying as I swam laps in the pool. Between breaths of air and gulps of water I prayed, *Lord, I know You have ways of turning bad things into something good, but I don't see anything good about our baby dying. Would You please help me see things from Your perspective?*

On the heels of that prayer, the idea of a book for other couples suffering the loss of a baby flashed across the screen of my mind. For the last several weeks I had searched bookstores trying to find something that would address my heartache. I found a couple of academic medical texts, but nothing that spoke to my emotional struggles or spiritual questions. This flash of an idea intrigued me. The graduate program in communications had sharpened my writing skills. I figured that if I could write a ninety-page thesis once, I could probably do it again on another topic of interest.

I sent a proposal and three sample chapters to six publishers. Two rejected the idea. One never responded. And three companies showed interest. I had lunch with a wonderful woman and skilled editor, Liz Heaney, who showed an unmatched excitement about the project. A year later Multnomah Publishers released my first book: *Empty Arms: Emotional Support for Those Who Have Experienced Miscarriage, Stillbirth or Tubal Pregnancy.* Liz did such a remarkable job helping me shape the book that it ended up being a Golden Medallion Award finalist. Do you know that little book has been on the market for sixteen years and is still being read by hundreds of grieving moms and dads each month?

God had a plan, and it was good.

The great news of publication brought about another Spring. The Lord led me back to graduate school to study psychology. Near the end of that two-year program we found out I was expecting again. I walked into my oral exams nine months pregnant. I think my profs took one look at me and felt sorry for the poor balloon of a woman in front of the class. I'm not sure if it was because I knew my material inside and out, or because they didn't want to create any undue stress that might trigger the onset of labor, but I breezed through my oral defense.

A week later our daughter, Jessie, was born. The years that followed were very happy. We enjoyed lighthearted days of Summer once again. Restoration and new life were springing up all around us. The congregation we were serving was healthy and growing. I had the luxury of working as a counselor two days a week and spending the rest of my time with Jessie and John.

Three years later our little Ben was born, and feeling complete, John and I decided the Vredevelt family would be "us four and no more." We were content with life, with our family, and with our ministry.

Then in 1991, it happened. I turned up pregnant. *How could it be?* I wondered. Well, I knew how it *could* be, but it shouldn't have been! We'd taken all the precautions. Somehow this baby was conceived in spite of the foolproof birth-control method we'd used for seventeen years. Life has a knack for teaching us that "control" is really an illusion.

When I was four months pregnant, I was speaking at a large women's conference at a hotel. One morning I had some time off, so I ordered breakfast in my room, read in the Gospel of John, and journaled my thoughts and feelings. I wrote and prayed all my frustration about being pregnant, my concerns about what the addition of another child would mean to our family life and schedule, and my uncertainty that I could handle what God was handing me. I can assure you, God got an earful.

But after I'd vented, it was His turn.

There have been times through the years when the Lord has made something very clear to me, and this was one of those times. As I was reading in John 15, I came across two familiar verses that jolted me like a double dose of smelling salts. Jesus was speaking: "I am the true vine, and my Father is the gardener. He cuts off every branch in me that bears no fruit, while every branch that does bear fruit he prunes so that it will be even more fruitful" (John 15:1–2).

What I sensed God saying to me was, "Pam, you're not being set back; you're being *cut* back."

And in that instant a picture of the three rosebushes in our front yard came to mind. Each summer the bushes produce huge, yellow, long-stemmed roses that fill our home with glorious fragrance. But in the fall, John cuts them back—way back. After his pruning shears do the job, I look at those stumps and think, *My goodness, the man is ruthless. Those poor things look decapitated!*

Every fall I wonder if they'll ever grow back, and sure enough, every spring they do. Little did I know, though, how deep the pruning shears would cut in my life.

Three months later our little Nathan was born, and John and I entered the harshest Winter we had yet encountered.

My days were filled with nursing a sick baby while trying to maintain some semblance of balance in the family. Some major decisions were necessary. I resigned from my job and cut back on some outside interests in order to use my energy and time to better tend to my family's needs. These sacrifices compounded my feelings of grief surrounding Nathan's diagnosis. (The detailed events of what God taught us during the next four years are chronicled in my book, *Angel Behind the Rocking Chair: Stories of Hope in Unexpected Places.*)

Those were difficult years. Certain treasures succumbed to the icy temperatures and died that Winter. I held some private funerals to commemorate personal losses:

- The death of the agenda for my life.
- The death of my dreams for a healthy baby.
- The death of a professional position.
- The death of creative writing for five years.
- The death of once-cherished areas of ministry.
- The death of much of my free time.
- The death of a few relationships due to lack of time and cultivation.

I even had times when my own soul felt dead.
But God had a plan, and it was good.
There is a fact of life: spring always follows winter. It's true for nature, and it's true for you and for me. God is always faithful to do what He says He will do.

I can honestly say that today, I am not the same woman I was before Nathan's arrival. New life is springing up everywhere through the sodden ashes of the old. I sense new vitality when I'm with John and the kids, in the counseling office, and on assignment where God leads. I have fresh confidence that I am where I am supposed to be at this time in my life. And if God wants me in a different place, I know He'll orchestrate circumstances to get me there.

The longer I walk with the Lord, the more convinced I am that God is impressed with only one thing: the life of His Spirit in us. God's chief aim is to make you and me more like Him. And, as the Master Gardener, He knows exactly when, where, and how deeply to prune so that His Spirit will take precedence in our lives.

There is nothing careless or arbitrary about the seasons we pass through. Each has its own brilliant colors, sights, and smells. With infinite creativity, a wise and loving God handpicks our seasons to teach us the mysteries of life, to put new songs on our lips, and to add depth and beauty to who we are. God, and God alone, knows best when to usher in a new season so that His Spirit can best accomplish His purposes. I am *convinced:* God has a plan, and it is good.

For me.

And for you.

Believe with me.

Power Perks: A Sip of Hope and Humor

Please do not stand there and talk, whine,
or ask questions. Wait until I get out.
Yes, it is locked. I want it that way.
It is not broken; I am not trapped.
I know I have left it unlocked,
and even open at times, since you were born,
because I was afraid some horrible tragedy
might occur while I was in there.
But it's been ten years, and I want some *privacy.*
Do not ask me how long I will be.
I will come out when I am done.
Do not bring the phone to the bathroom door.
Do not go running back to the phone yelling,
"She's in the *bathroom!*"
Do not begin to fight as soon as I go in.
Do not stick your little fingers under the
door and wiggle them.
This was funny only when you were two.
Do not slide pennies, Legos, or notes under the door.
Even when you were two, this got a little tiresome.
If you have followed me down the hall, talking,
and are still talking as you face this closed door,
please turn around, walk away,
and wait for me in another room.
I will be glad to listen to you when I am done.
Oh…and yes, I still love you.
Mom

In this life we will encounter hurts and trials that we will not be able
to change; we are just going to have to let them change us.

Ron Lee Davis[1]

CHAPTER 5

Sowing Hope's Seeds

I will open up the windows of heaven for you
and pour out a blessing so great
you won't have room enough to take it in!

Malachi 3:10, TLB

What wish lays silent, unmoving, in your heart today? Do you have a dream that is all vapor, no reality? Have you almost given up hope that it will see sunlight?

Come, meet my friend Laurel. A musician by trade, she and I met quite by "accident" on a flight to Southern California. When she told me her story, I wanted to share it with you. Laurel, you see, knows the weight of wanting something and having to trust God for it. She also knows the power God gives to small steps taken in the right direction. I'll let her explain.

"Laurel, what is your heart's desire?"

When a friend asked me that, I was stunned for a moment. I really had never given the concept a thought. From the day my husband, Steve, and I walked the marriage aisle, we had been laying down our lives to share God's love with others through music. It was a dream with a demand: We experienced the deep joy of living sacrificially, but we also lived out of suitcases. That was fairly easy when our family just consisted of Steve and me; but when we added two sons, it was chaotic.

So after ten years of troubadour life, when my friend asked me what I really wanted, I felt selfish but admitted, "I want a house and roots." When I said that, I waded back through memories to the old mouse-house we lived in after our second son was born. I was still reeling from the claustrophobic, four-hundred-square-foot apartment we had occupied when we were on a music assignment in Japan. There simply wasn't enough room for us with our newborn baby and very active four-year-old. By the time we returned to the United States, I was tuckered out, fed up, and not convinced we were successful on our mission. Frankly, I found it quite difficult to dream.

The thought of having my own home, with a yard and swing set for the kids, seemed like an impossibility. But my friends prayed anyway.

Two days later our phone rang. Our neighbors across the

street announced that they were moving and that their landlords were going to sell the house. That got my attention. I loved the house. It was modest, yet pretty; small, yet nicely laid out for a family of four. And it was much larger than the home we were currently renting. I told my neighbor we were interested.

That started "the talks." The owner said he was open to a lease-option so that we could have time to save for a down payment. We were off to a good start. Then we made an offer. He turned us down. As we waited for a counteroffer, every day we witnessed a parade of potential buyers passing in front of "our" home. I could tell they were people with options. Down payments. Steady jobs.

We thought about ways we could discourage potential buyers. We were tempted to put a rusty, beat-up car in our driveway. We considered staging some knock-down-drag-out fights on the front lawn. But we chose to mind our manners.

One afternoon my mom brought over a gift for me. She knew I was depressed and thought a bucket of tulip bulbs, ready for planting, would cheer me up. It didn't—at first. I took one look at the bucket and thought, *Why would I want to plant these beautiful flowers in this ramshackle rental house when I really want to live in that house across the street?*

Then I answered my own question. I marched across the street with shovel, gloves, and bulbs in hand. One by one, I placed those little bulbs in the ground, praying over each one, and asked God to unfold His plan in our lives. My spirit started to lift. I sang, dug holes, and patted the dirt into place, oblivious to the world around me.

A gruff voice startled me. "What are you doin' there, little missy?"

"I'm planting flowers," I responded, wiping my brow.

"But don'tcha live in that house over there?" he asked, pointing across the street.

"Yes, but…well, I want to live in this one."

He walked away, shaking his head, muttering. I resumed my task. Hope still sang, quietly, in my heart.

A week later the owner showed up at our door with a counteroffer. The amount sounded doable, but there was a catch. We had to come up with the down payment in three months. I gasped. After the owner left, I closed the door, leaned against the wall, and thought, *No way. There is no possible way on this earth that we can get that much money that fast.*

Steve begged to differ. (Steve has the spiritual gift of faith. I have the gift of suspicion.) He said we should accept the offer, move in, and trust God to provide what we needed. A week later we trotted all of our belongings across the street and settled into our new home.

As the three-month deadline approached, I started to panic. We had saved our pennies to the best of our ability, but there still wasn't enough, and we didn't have any gigs on the calendars. Prayers upheld us.

Early one morning, when the deadline was one week away, the phone rang. Someone I hadn't talked with in years was on the other end of the line, wanting to know what I was doing that weekend. I told her I didn't have any plans.

"Great!" she said. "Would you lead the singing at the Women of Faith conference this weekend in Tacoma?"

"Would I? Are you kidding? I'd love to lead the music for those ladies!" We made all the necessary plans. When I hung up the phone, I realized I was so excited about being involved with the conference that I hadn't even asked about the compensation.

The weekend was a gift from heaven. Leading the women in song after song of praise to God brought my focus back to what mattered most. The lyrics refreshed my soul. I thoroughly enjoyed getting to know the women teaching the conference. And, as soon as the teaching sessions were over, hundreds of ladies flocked through the auditorium doors in a mad dash to the various music and book tables. I was absolutely overwhelmed by the women's eagerness to buy my CD. In all my concert tours, I had never experienced anything like it.

When I returned home, Steve and I tallied up the CD sales, the honorarium, and the money we had set aside in savings. By now, you've probably guessed the end of the story. God had provided exactly what we needed.

To this day, whenever I see a tulip in bloom, I remember a time when my dreams were lost in a fog of fatigue and perceived failure. But God, through the encouragement of my praying friends, an unexpected opportunity, and a bucket of tulips, resurrected those dreams and then brought them to pass. I shouldn't be surprised—one of God's names is Jehovah Jireh, which means "the God who provides."

In the midst of her dormant dream, Laurel made an important decision. She acted on her goal and put feet on her frustration. When she planted those tulips in the yard of her dream house, she planted her desires in God's hands. She invited Him to work. And hope sprouted.

What small step can you take today toward what you hope for? It need be nothing more outrageous than planting a flower bulb in an empty lot. But it's an act with meaning. Plant a dream seed today.

Power Perks: A Sip of Hope and Humor

I know of a gynecologist who is not only deaf, but blind as well. He telephoned a friend of mine who is also a physician in the practice of obstetrics and gynecology. He asked for a favor.

"My wife has been having some abdominal discomfort this afternoon," he said. "I don't want to treat my own wife and wonder if you would see her for me?"

My friend invited the doctor to bring his wife for an examination, whereupon he discovered (are you ready for this?) that she was five months pregnant! Her obstetrician husband was so busy caring for other patients that he hadn't even noticed his wife's burgeoning pregnancy. I must admit wondering how in the world this woman ever got his attention long enough to conceive![1]

I heard about a woman who confused her Valium with her birth control pills. She had fourteen kids, but she doesn't much care.

God needs no one, but when faith is present He works through anyone.

A. W. Tozer[2]

To have faith is to believe the task ahead of us is never as great as the Power behind us.[3]

We never test the resources of God until we attempt the impossible.

F. B. Meyer[4]

There is surely a future hope for you, and your hope will not be cut off.
Proverbs 23:18

CHAPTER 6

A Fresh Touch

The people brought children to Jesus, hoping he might touch them. The disciples shooed them off. But Jesus was irate and let them know it: "Don't push these children away. Don't ever get between them and me. These children are at the very center of life in the kingdom." Then, gathering the children up in his arms, he laid his hands of blessing on them.

Mark 10:13–14, 16, MSG

It was one of those weeks. It had been filled with the typical demands of the children's school and sports activities, their homework, my counseling responsibilities, taxi driving, and daily household chores. But complicating our routine was the lack of a certain essential member: John was in Honduras, ministering for eight days, and my-oh-my, did I miss him. By the end of the fifth day, I was pooped.

I honestly don't know how single moms do it. I have tremendous respect for their tenacity and perseverance in the midst of overwhelming pressures. When John is gone, I get a jarring reality check about how important he is to me and the children—and how much of the family load he carries. The wheels of the clan definitely turn more smoothly when we work together as a team.

The kids feel it, too. They have built-in radar that detects with 100 percent accuracy when I'm worn thin. I suppose it's human nature, but when Dad's away, they seem to step up their efforts to divide and conquer. They get squirrelly and try to push the limits in ways that wouldn't even cross their minds when Dad is home.

I weathered my fair share of their conniving and cajoling the week John was in Honduras. Everyone acted up somehow, but Nathan won the Pressing Mom to the Limit prize. It had been months since Nathan's last escape, and we actually thought he might have outgrown his disappearing acts. But while John was out of the country, Nathan managed to slip out of the house unnoticed not once, not twice, but *three* times.

He pulled his first disappearing act when I thought he was in his bedroom with his brother, Ben, playing Nintendo. I was enjoying a fresh cup of coffee at the kitchen table and writing a letter when the doorbell rang. Glancing out the front window, I saw an unfamiliar car in our driveway and wondered who would be dropping by early Saturday morning. When I opened the door, a woman who lived down the street stood there with Nathan in tow.

"Is this your little boy?" she inquired. I stammered that he was.

The story unfolded. "I was driving along Eastman Parkway [the main access road a block from our home], and I saw him running down the street. So I stopped my car, asked him to get in, and brought him back."

I couldn't believe it. I thanked this angel of a neighbor, whose name I didn't even know, for taking the time to rescue Nathan. After she left I about lost my breakfast. All the "what ifs" closed in on me. Initially all I could do was wrap my arms tightly around Nathan and hug him close. I was so grateful no harm had come to him. After my heart stopped racing, I talked sternly with Nathan about the dangers of leaving the house without his mommy or daddy. Then he took a very l-o-n-g time-out on the kitchen stool.

After Nathan paid his penance, I asked him to show me how he escaped. He led me downstairs to the basement back door. The evidence was plentiful. There, by the door, was the chair from my office rolled into perfect position so that he could climb high enough to release the latch we use for extra security.

I plopped down on the chair, leaned my head back against the door with a sigh of resignation, and wondered, *Now what are we going to do?* As my imagination went wild I thought aloud,

"How about an electronic tracking device? Or how about a computer chip implant with radar-detection capabilities?"

I know. It was one of my more neurotic moments. But when you're desperate, all kinds of strange things seem rational.

I wish I could say that the trouble stopped there. But I began getting notes from Nathan's teacher: "I don't know what's going on with Nathan, but he isn't himself lately." He wasn't transitioning well from one activity to the next, and he didn't want to participate in things he typically enjoyed. Since Nathan is able to communicate with only a few words, it's often hard to know the source of his frustrations. What he can't say he usually acts out.

But I discerned what was going on. He hadn't seen his dad for several days, and for him things just weren't right. He was used to John's daily presence. He was used to hugs in the morning and evening and high fives through the day. He was used to showing his dad his picture chart from school that detailed his daily activities. Smiling and frowning faces defined his behavior during the day. His dad praised and affirmed every smiley face. And when Nathan sheepishly pointed to the frowns, his dad encouraged him: "Nathan, tomorrow you can make a better choice. Tomorrow you can line up at recess and follow your teacher's instructions. Bring me home a smiley face from recess, okay, Nathan?"

"Okay, Dada."

When my concerns about Nathan seemed about to erupt into total frustration, John came home. Thank God! At the dinner table he told us about two orphanages he visited in Honduras. They were full of little boys and girls who had been abandoned to the streets of Tegucigalpa. He spent the week assessing their needs so that later in the year he could take our family back along with a team from the church to help. The experience moved him to tears: "I'll never forget the way those little kids grabbed onto me when I visited them. They nearly cut off the circulation in my legs. They were so starved for affection, it was like they were hanging on for dear life."

In some ways, I realized, Nathan is—and you and I are—like the children in the Honduran orphanage. When we are disconnected from our Father, there is a feeling that something isn't right. We act in ways that aren't like us. We look for back doors so we can escape from our internal chaos. We grab onto false sources of security, hoping to satisfy our deepest longings. We try to fill the hole in our soul with people, position, power, pleasure, pills.

But what we really need is what Nathan needed—and what the children in Honduras couldn't get enough of. We need a fresh touch from our Father.

A touch of His peace, which isn't remotely disrupted by the surprises life delivers us.

A touch of His joy, which can transcend our disappointments.

A touch of His wisdom, which often defies human reasoning.

A touch of His grace, which has the power to wash away our guilt.

A touch of His stubborn love, which embraces us as we are, while challenging us to become all we can be.

A touch of His resurrection power, which can revive the dead places in our soul.

The day after John returned, Nathan hopped off the bus, waving his picture chart for all to see. John pulled him up on his knee, and the three of us reviewed the day. Nine smiley faces and two frowns—a drastic improvement over the five previous reports! The following day was even better. *All* the faces wore happy smiles. It's amazing what some time with Dad can do.

How is your week going? Are you a little out of sync? Feeling on the edge of fragmented? Are you wearing more frowns than smiles? Why not schedule some time alone with your heavenly Father? You'll never know how much your report card can improve until you do.

Power Perks: A Sip of Hope and Humor

Two ladies were traveling with a busload of sight-seeing senior citizens on a trip to Honduras. As they approached the town of Tegucigalpa, they started arguing about how to pronounce the name of the city. Back and forth they bantered until the bus driver interrupted and announced that it was time to stop for lunch.

At the local restaurant, they stepped up to the counter, reviewed the menu, and waited for the waitress to take their order. When the young lady behind the counter asked, "Can I help you?" one of the women said, "Yes. Could you please help us settle an argument?"

The waitress shrugged and asked, "What's the problem?"

"Could you please pronounce very clearly where we are?" one of the women responded.

At that point the young woman leaned forward, and with purposeful, well-defined articulation, said: "Tah-ko-bell."

Warmth, friendliness, and a gentle touch are always stronger than force and fury.

Denis Waitley[1]

Can't you see the Creator of the universe, who understands every secret, every mystery…sitting patiently and listening to a four-year-old talk to Him? That's a beautiful image of a father.

James Dobson[2]

You fathers—if your children ask for a fish, do you give them a snake instead? Or if they ask for an egg, do you give them a scorpion? Of course not! If you sinful people know how to give good gifts to your children, how much more will your heavenly Father give the Holy Spirit to those who ask him.

Luke 11:11–13, NLT

CHAPTER 7

Pooped Out by Perfectionism

[Jesus said:] "Are you tired? Worn out? Burned out on religion? Come to me. Get away with me and you'll recover your life. I'll show you how to take a real rest. Walk with me and work with me— watch how I do it. Learn the unforced rhythms of grace. I won't lay anything heavy or ill-fitting on you. Keep company with me and you'll learn to live freely and lightly."

Matthew 11:28–30, MSG

When Marti came to me for counseling, she appeared to have, as the old song says, the world on a string. Marti, you see, looked as if she stepped off the pages of a fashion magazine. She was a six-foot flashy brunette with piercing blue eyes. She had the bone structure women covet and the naturally lustrous hair beauty salons can't re-create. I'm not exaggerating in the slightest when I say she was gorgeous.

Aside from her physical beauty, Marti also had poise—a refined stride from years of ballet and modeling and an elegance in her mannerisms. Of course Marti also had a marvelous sense of style; she wore the finest garb from international boutiques around the world. Her makeup was applied and her hair styled to perfection.

In short, Marti had it all. The casual observer would likely conclude she didn't have a care in the world. After all, life had dealt Marti a winning hand.

Or had it?

Appearances aren't everything, are they? On the outside this twenty-nine-year-old was Madison Avenue picture-perfect. But on the inside...well, nothing was in order. This beauty queen was also a slave—to the tyrannical taskmaster of perfectionism.

At home Marti was the mother of two toddlers who ran her ragged. Her entire life revolved around these whirlwinds who demanded her constant attention. Consequently Marti's house reflected the pandemonium of her mind. No matter how hard she tried, it was always a mess. Toys were everywhere. Cereal littered the floor from kitchen to living room, and juice spots dotted the bedroom carpet. Not even the garage was safe—the clutter seemed to find nesting places in every inch surrounding the car.

Perhaps the biggest surprise of all was that despite her natural beauty and sophisticated style, Marti hated the way she looked. She felt tired and droopy and dragged herself through each day. At night there was little rest for this weary woman who lay awake for hours, unable to close the day with sleep.

Unfortunately, she didn't get much relief from her husband, Don. This worn-out woman hadn't been anywhere exciting with her husband for years. The big event of her week was when Don watched the little monsters (oops—I mean *precious pumpkins*) after work while Marti went to the grocery store. The lovely woman sitting across from me was depressed, anxious, and above all, defeated. Marti felt completely insufficient in her capacities as a mother and wife.

When Marti came to me, she was afraid that if she didn't get some help, she was going to strangle the kids. Well, there's nothing like a couple of toddling tornadoes to expose—and challenge—the perfectionism in a person's character. But my, how everyone suffers in the process. Physical exhaustion exacerbated her frustration. The more inadequate Marti felt, the harder she tried. She stayed up until the wee hours of the morning scrubbing the kitchen, rearranging toy shelves, and cleaning closets. She desperately needed rest, but in her quest for the perfect home, she was too driven to slow down.

Marti and I started talking about how rigid thinking patterns fueled her frenzy. Her view of life was black and white: the kids were either perfect angels or diabolical brats. She was either a wonder woman or a total deadbeat. Her house was either

Sunset-magazine impeccable or a demolition zone. In every area of her life, she was either triumphing or failing—there was no middle ground, no "good enough." And naturally, she gave herself an F for effort.

I sensed that there were issues beneath the surface that ignited Marti's perfectionism. After all, it's a pattern we learn over time—most of us aren't born a perfectionist. As we worked together over several months, the truth emerged.

When Marti was five years old, an uncle had sexually abused her. Now that Marti had children of her own, she was terrified of leaving them with anyone. From the day her kids were born, they had always been in either Marti or Don's care. Fear had a death grip on this poor woman.

Her obsession with her kids' safety led to their control in the home. Thus all of Marti's energies went toward keeping the kids happy and in sight while the household fell to pieces. In her mind, the untidy home was evidence of another responsibility she couldn't handle.

Marti's perfectionism was a coping response to childhood trauma. It was her attempt to control the internal chaos triggered by the loss of her innocence and the violation of her body and soul. Her parents had nurtured the perfectionism as well. They gave Marti attention and approval when she did something outstanding but withdrew their love when she performed less than perfectly. Desperate to win her parents' love, Marti strove relentlessly to excel in all she did. She was a model achiever. But underneath the apparently flawless surface were deep insecurities and a perpetual anxiety.

During our sessions together Marti bravely confronted her worst fears about her children being harmed. She began to see that the coping skills she used to survive as a child were impairing the quality of her life as an adult. She learned that she had the power to make other choices. She could set boundaries. She could say no. She could openly acknowledge and grieve her losses and let them go.

In time Marti gained the courage to take some chances. She and her husband talked about establishing a date night. After a few trial runs, Marti and Don took the plunge. They went to dinner a couple of miles from home and returned to find the babysitter on the couch with both children on her lap, happily reading *The Cat in the Hat.*

The kids had survived.

Marti had survived.

And her marriage had taken a major step forward.

Date nights are now a regular part of Marti and Don's routine. And in general the kids have settled down. It doesn't surprise me. When Mom is living within healthy boundaries, and she and Dad are in sync, the kids sense it and respond well to security and order.

Marti and I spent a number of months together, and I had a front-row seat in watching her become more comfortable with the "good enough" in life. She worked hard at lowering the bar for herself and her kids. She learned the art of affirming herself for efforts made toward a given goal. Now and then she even gives herself permission to do an "average" job on household tasks instead of shooting for an A-plus on everything. Her motto is "Practice makes better, not perfect."

Really, there is nothing perfect this side of heaven. Yet that is the standard many feel called to, isn't it? I remember as a college student reading some words spoken by Jesus: "You are to be perfect, even as your Father in heaven is perfect" (Matthew 5:48, TLB). That verse really bugged me. I thought God was saying, "Pam, there is no margin for error. You've got to strive to be perfect." But I knew full well I could never achieve that. The assignment was completely unrealistic. So I sighed, closed my Bible, and chose to forget it. That was twenty years ago.

Recently I was reading through the book of Matthew. When I came to this verse, for the first time I saw it in a bigger context. The message suddenly made more sense to me.

There is a saying, "Love your *friends* and hate your enemies." But I say: Love your *enemies!* Pray for those who *persecute* you! In that way you will be acting as true sons of your Father in heaven. For he gives his sunlight to both the evil and the good, and sends rain on the just and on the unjust too. If you love only those who love you, what good is that? Even scoundrels do that much.

If you are friendly only to your friends, how are you different from anyone else? Even the heathen do that. But you are to be perfect, even as your Father in heaven is perfect. (Matthew 5:43–48, TLB)

The theme of this text is love given unconditionally. Such an approach to relationships flies in the face of any demand for behavioral perfection first. The verses say to me, "Pam, you are to love your husband and children and friends without condition. Not because they are perfect. Not because they do what you want. Not because they measure up to your expectations or please you. You are to love them unconditionally because that is the way God loves you."

I did some digging into the meaning of the word *perfect*. In the context of this Scripture passage, I learned, the word actually means *mature*. That's very different from *flawless* or *without error*. What Jesus is suggesting is that we love maturely, the way God does. We are to stop approving of ourselves and others only when things are done "right." Mature love isn't tangled up in the demand for failure-free living. It isn't bound by an overriding sense of perfectionism. It is based in freedom.

As Marti learned, perfectionism is an inner drive to live up to a man-made standard. Maturity is loving God, others, and ourselves regardless of whether or not these standards are met. Unconditional love breaks the power of perfectionism into a million and one irretrievable pieces. It allows the process of growth to develop and establishes a foundation of freedom—even to fail—in our lives.

Will you join me in passing on some unconditional love today? It's a tall assignment, I know, one that requires supernatural help. But the One with the espresso for your spirit is ready to fill your cup. To overflowing.

And you know, when there are peace and love on the inside, the outside can't help but reflect it. That's what I call true beauty. It's the kind Marti exudes today.

Power Perks: A Sip of Hope and Humor

I have measured my life in coffee spoons.

T. S. Eliot[1]

A woman was terribly overweight, so her doctor put her on a diet. "I want you to eat regularly for two days, then skip a day, and repeat this procedure for two weeks. The next time I see you, you'll have lost at least five pounds."

When the woman returned, she'd lost nearly twenty pounds. "Why, that's amazing!" the doctor said. "Did you follow my instructions?"

The woman nodded. "I'll tell you, though, I thought I was going to drop dead that third day."

"From hunger, you mean?"

"No, from skipping."

They keep telling us to get in touch with our bodies. Mine isn't all that communicative, but I heard from it the other day. When I said, "Body, how would you like to go to the six o'clock class in vigorous toning?" Clear as a bell it replied, "You do it—you die!"

He who is faultless is lifeless.

John Heywood[2]

The farther a man knows himself to be from perfection, the nearer he is to it.

Gerard Groote[3]

CHAPTER 8

What an Inheritance!

God's Spirit touches our spirits and confirms who we really are. We know who he is, and we know who we are: Father and children. And we know we are going to get what's coming to us—an unbelievable inheritance!

Romans 8:16–17, MSG

As a therapist I'm intrigued by the concept of change. I like to know what motivates people to alter their actions and attitudes—and how they maintain those changes. As a woman who counsels primarily women, I'm curious about the female heritage in a family tree—why some ladies seem to model their mothers' mindsets while others seem completely different from those who raised them.

My friend Diane is a woman who happens to be very different from the matriarchs of former generations. Yet I see striking similarities between Diane and her grown daughter, Nikki. Both are strong leaders. Both give themselves sacrificially to their family and friends. Both love God and mankind without embarrassment or reserve.

One afternoon I was able to snatch a sneak peak into Diane's past. It became obvious to me that she had purposely made some significant choices that had made her a healthy, sturdy oak in her family tree. I asked her to tell her story.

I never thought much about the legacy I received from my mother and grandmother until my own daughter was eight years old. It was then that I grew increasingly concerned over some alarming traits that seemed to be surfacing in her character. I kept hearing her toss out negative barbs about people in her class. There was a sharp edge to her voice. That's when it dawned on me: My grandma was critical. My mother was critical. And now Nikki was critical.

Somehow, I thought, *that nasty critical curse skipped right over me and went on to my daughter.* I wish! Isn't it amazing how easy it is to see the speck in someone else's eye and not recognize the log in our own? The Lord began to help me see the part I was playing in passing this not-so-positive inheritance on to Nikki.

I recalled a verse of Scripture that I had known for years: "I will bring the curse of a father's sins upon even the third and fourth generation of the children of those who hate me; but I will show kindness to a thousand generations of those who love me and keep my commandments" (Deuteronomy 5:9–10, TLB). It was clear from these verses that God's greatest desire was to bless us and our children and the generations to come. But I didn't know how to put an end to the patterns that had filtered down through our generations in order to begin receiving the blessings God intended for us.

I talked with Nikki about the critical spirit I observed in my grandmother, my mother, myself, and her. Together we decided that we were going to stop that curse from traveling any further down our bloodline. Even though Nikki was only eight at the time, she fully understood and wanted to make things different. I asked her to forgive me for being overly critical toward her, and then I led her in a simple prayer. *Lord, Nikki and I don't want to have a critical spirit. We want to be different from the way we have been in the past. Please forgive us for being judgmental and hard on others, and help us to be careful with what comes out of our mouths. Together we make a statement today that this curse will no longer influence our lives. In Jesus' name, amen.*

From that day on we resolved to help each other remember to stay positive so we wouldn't slip into old habits. For a season, this worked. But then, at times, it seemed like we were back at square one. Over time I discovered an ugly thread of criticism weaving its way in and out of my thoughts and conversations.

And I hated it. But the more I tried not to be critical, the worse my thoughts became.

Battle fatigue set in, and I finally realized this was not a war I was going to win on my own. I got back down on my knees and asked God to help me. I sensed His reassurance and heard Him say, "Diane, I don't give you power to 'not do something.' I give you power to be who I've called you to be."

Who have You called me to be, Lord?

Galatians 5 came to mind. I opened my Bible and there before my eyes was the answer I needed:

> But when the Holy Spirit controls our lives he will produce this kind of fruit in us: love, joy, peace, patience, kindness, goodness, faithfulness, gentleness and self-control.... If we are living now by the Holy Spirit's power, let us follow the Holy Spirit's leading in every part of our lives. (Galatians 5:22–23, 25, TLB)

With a renewed sense of hope, I gave the Spirit of God permission to be my teacher. To teach me how to be gracious. To show me how to believe the best in others. To help me to see through eyes of love and compassion as He sees. I asked God to teach me the lessons that had never been modeled for me when I was growing up.

Above all, I stopped trying to stop being critical. I tried instead to be full of the fruit of God's Spirit. What a difference that made! I no longer had to try to drive forward while looking in a rearview mirror. I was no longer limited by the emotional and relational impoverishment of the past. The Holy Spirit was capable of guiding me in a new approach to life.

Bit by bit, God took hold of my natural bent and the twisted portions of my upbringing and straightened them out. He helped me cultivate the habit of looking for others' strengths instead of their weaknesses. He prompted me to assume the best instead of the worst. It was a long process, but in time caution gave way to kindness. Suspicion gave way to support. I became less tentative and more trusting. To this day, whenever I hear people say, "Diane, you are very gracious," I usually chuckle and whisper a prayer of thanks.

Nikki, too, has experienced success. Friends and relations speak of her as one of the most sweet-spirited women they know. I believe Nikki's character shines in this specific way because I purposely chose to deal with my own critical bent and modeled a desire for change in front of Nikki. She followed my lead, and together we persevered through the process of transformation. As we did our part, God did His. Nikki and I saw in dramatic ways that nothing is more powerful than a divinely inspired idea put into practice consistently.

Nikki and I knelt in prayer together nearly twenty years ago, asking God to replace our critical spirits with more of His Holy Spirit. Our persistent plodding toward reducing the negatives and increasing the positives in our conversations paid off. Holding each other accountable kept us moving forward too. I can honestly say today that God has done a good work in me and in my daughter.

———

Today, thanks to a tenacious desire to grow good fruit from imperfect roots, Diane and Nikki have transformed a deadly family trait into a beautiful, life-giving legacy. They have sprouted a quality that will be much in demand for generations to come. With an inheritance like that, I can guarantee one thing: The blessings are going to go on and on and on.

Power Perks: A Sip of Hope and Humor

The last proof that coffee or tea is favorable to intellectual expression is that all nations use one or the other as aids to conversation.

Philip G. Hamerton[1]

———

They say the typical symptoms of stress are eating too much chocolate, drinking too much coffee, spending too much time shopping, and sleeping too many hours a day. Are they kidding? Sounds like a perfect day to me.

———

Woman who beef too much find herself in stew.

Chinese Proverb[2]

———

People who are always pointing fingers rarely hold out their hands.[3]

———

Criticism leaves you with the flattering unction that you are a superior person. It is impossible to develop the characteristics of a saint and maintain a critical attitude.

Oswald Chambers[4]

———

Whom you would change, you must first love.

Martin Luther King Jr.[5]

CHAPTER 9

The Power of Percolating Prayers

ou can make many plans, but the LORD's purpose will prevail.

Proverbs 19:21, NLT

Have you ever prayed a percolating prayer? You know, one that is short on words but heavy on pleading? I introduced this concept in *Espresso for Your Spirit: Hope and Humor for Pooped Out Parents.* These are brief yet power-packed prayers that make the important connection between a needy human and a powerful God.

My friend Wendy offered this prayer one night: *What do I need to do, Lord? We are so very far from what You want. I have been praying for months, but very little seems to change. God, You've got to intervene and help us.*

And that is exactly what our faithful Father did. Not in a way Wendy would have anticipated. And definitely not in a way she would have chosen. But in a way that worked. Let me share her amazing story.

———

Dear Jesus, please watch over Mama Darla. And watch over Timmy, Tommy, Jake, and JoJo, and Grandma and Grandpa....

Wendy's heart sank when she heard Bethany, her adopted daughter, pray for her "other" family—again. It had been nearly a year since she and Laurence had welcomed this fragile ten-year-old into their hearts and home. During daytime hours Wendy frequently heard, "I love you, Mom," but at night, when Bethany talked to her heavenly Father, her thoughts were focused on her birth family. Wendy understood the yearnings of this little one's heart but longed for Bethany to pray for her new family, too.

Laurence and Wendy had first met Bethany's birth mother, Darla, fourteen years before. Darla lived with the couple now and then while trying to break free from a drug addiction. Life eventually took the two families in different directions, but through the years Darla occasionally brought Bethany and her boys to visit. Then one afternoon Darla unexpectedly called Laurence and Wendy with a startling request: "Wendy, my parental rights are being terminated by the state. The other kids are settled, but would you please consider taking Bethany? I haven't been able to get you off my mind."

At the time Laurence and Wendy were close to having an empty nest. Of their three daughters, only the youngest, nineteen-year-old Michelle, was still at home. The couple traveled frequently and was involved in a marriage ministry at their church. They wondered how they could give up their comfort and open their hearts to a child with such deep emotional scars. Their home would be Bethany's eighth.

Everything in them resisted the idea. But it was impossible to shake Bethany from their thoughts. So they prayed.

One evening while Wendy was considering the implications of the adoption, the Lord spoke to her, saying: "You will become complete when you have this little girl by your side. You will find great joy in helping Bethany heal."

Wendy understood what God was saying. She had already spent many years processing the pain of her own childhood wounds. She sensed God reassuring her that Bethany would be a catalyst for new expressions of health and joy in their family. Wendy loved being a mom and had always wanted four children. She saw Bethany's coming as the fulfillment of that dream. When the rest of the family promised their support, Wendy and Laurence were convinced.

As the couple filled out the application and took adoption classes, the waiting period felt much like a typical pregnancy. Wendy's mind was consumed with thoughts of their new addition. She found her love for Bethany growing with each passing day. Finally the call came: "They said yes!" Laurence jubilantly declared. "Bethany is ours!"

They drove to the foster home where Bethany was staying. Bethany ran straight into Wendy's arms. Wendy squeezed the thin little girl in a warm embrace. Bethany turned to Laurence and said, "Hi, Dad." Their journey to becoming a family had begun.

Within the week, Bethany moved all of her belongings into Laurence and Wendy's home. The honeymoon phase was wonderful. Joy bubbled within Wendy. "I love having another daughter!" she told Laurence. "Bethany is going to keep us young!"

Yet the couple knew from the adoption classes that the honeymoon phase would be followed by a time of testing. In one way or another adoptive children are compelled to ask, "Will you still want me when you see what I am really like?" They usually seek answers through acting out.

You've probably had the experience of trying to focus on one big challenge when you're hit with another. This is what Wendy and Laurence experienced. A few short weeks after Bethany had settled into her new home, Laurence's father died unexpectedly. Wendy and Laurence had to fly to New Zealand for the funeral while Bethany stayed with their two older daughters.

The disruption brought to the surface Bethany's overwhelming fear of abandonment. "Don't go, Mom! Please don't go!" she cried, clinging to Wendy. Wendy's heart was torn, but she knew she needed to be with her husband.

When the couple returned from New Zealand, school began and so did a jarring season of testing. Anger began to haunt the household. Explosions and tears became frequent. Time-outs became a daily occurrence for all of them because they needed breaks from each other to calm down and think straight. Wendy felt as if her parenting skills had evaporated. The conflicts were so frequent that she and Laurence wondered if they had made the right decision.

When they sent Bethany to her room, she wrote them letters. On a good day, the letter might read:

Dear Mom,
I'm sorry I was a very naughty girl tonight. I still love you. Please forgive me.
From Bethany Dunn

On a bad day, the letter might read:

Wendy. I want help. Can you help? Will you help?
Check yes/no.

Wendy felt as if a knife pierced her heart when Bethany called her "Wendy" instead of "Mom." Bethany's comments about wanting to live with Darla again when she was eighteen twisted the knife even deeper. Wendy wondered if the little girl would ever accept her new family.

Around the time her first grandchild was born, some perpetual pains in Wendy's abdomen could be ignored no longer. She made an appointment with her doctor, whose words were brief and blunt: "You have a large mass on one of your ovaries, Wendy. We have to consider the possibility of cancer."

In shock, Wendy spent the following weekend cuddling her new grandbaby. "We *do* have a future together," she whispered to little Whitney. Throughout the weekend, whenever Wendy looked at Bethany, she prayed: *God, I don't believe You sent her to me just to have her lose another mother.*

As the tense meetings with doctors and the excruciating waiting periods for test results took their toll, Wendy sank into depression. Percolating prayers became the only kind she could pray as she worried over her family, especially its newest member: *God, I don't have what I need to be Bethany's mother! My energy is completely gone. I can't deal with her or anyone else right now.*

A family from church took Bethany home while Wendy prepared for surgery. Amazingly, the hospitalization was a peace-filled experience. She felt the prayers of dozens of friends around the world. She sensed God's assurance that "this is not for death—this is for life," and she was confident that He was directing their steps.

Wendy went into surgery. As she emerged from the anesthesia she heard Laurence say, "Yes, it is cancer. But it was caught early. You are going to be all right." Cushioned by God's love, Wendy felt no fear.

Recovery from the surgery, however, seemed to take forever. Under doctor's orders Wendy was confined to the basement of her home to avoid stairs for two weeks. She hated being separated from the rest of the family and less available to meet Bethany's emotional needs.

One day during this period, Wendy's daughter Sharyn came to visit and assist around the house. That afternoon Wendy heard Bethany's agitated voice upstairs, then crying and shouting. Stuck in the basement, Wendy sent up a few more percolating prayers through her tears.

"It's all my fault my family broke up!" Bethany screamed. "It's all my fault!"

Wendy heard Sharyn trying to comfort the little girl. She asked gently, "Bethany, are you afraid something bad will happen to our family, too?"

"No way!" Bethany said. "This family will never fall apart! It's like one person. Each of you is like one part of that person. Even if someone doesn't do his share, the rest of you work together to help that person."

Is that what this is all about? Wendy whispered to her heavenly Father. *Are You trying to teach Bethany that a family doesn't have to fall apart even under terrible pressures?*

The answer came over the next few months as Wendy underwent chemotherapy and found herself too ill and exhausted to contribute much to the family. One day she told Bethany, "I'm so sorry that I can't do things with you like I want to."

In a surprisingly soft voice, Bethany answered, "That's okay,

Mom. I know you can't help being sick."

Bethany began growing into an understanding and generous child. It seemed that Wendy's suffering brought out the best in the little girl. She adjusted to her place in the household, doing her chores without complaint and helping Wendy in any way she could. The harsh circumstances the family was enduring forced Bethany to focus on others instead of herself.

A long, difficult year passed. Wendy was declared free from cancer. And just as wonderful, though Bethany continued to be challenged by the issues of her past, the major issue was settled: She knew she was family. Though there were still conflicts, Bethany began to regularly display love and affection and made more efforts to cooperate.

Through it all, Wendy and Bethany have grown close. This was never more apparent than at bedtime when she tucked Bethany in and heard her prayers: *Dear God, please watch over Mom. Help her to have a good night's sleep and to feel better in the morning. Help her get well. And please, God, watch over my dad, too.*

Wendy's prayers changed, too: *Dear Heavenly Father, please be with Bethany's Mama Darla wherever she is tonight and comfort her. Be with Timmy, Tommy, Jake, and JoJo. And most of all, dear Lord, continue to have Your way in all of our lives. Amen.*

Power Perks: A Sip of Hope and Humor

The Top Ten Things to Say If You
Get Caught Sleeping at Your Desk

10. "They told me at the blood bank that this might happen."
 9. "This is just a fifteen-minute power nap like they raved about in that time-management course you sent me to."
 8. "Whew! Guess I left the top off the correction fluid. You probably got here just in time!"
 7. "I wasn't sleeping! I was meditating on our mission statement and envisioning a new paradigm."
 6. "I was testing my keyboard for drool resistance."
 5. "I was doing a highly specific yoga exercise to relieve work-related stress. Do you discriminate against people who practice yoga?"
 4. "Why did you interrupt me? I had almost figured out a solution to our biggest problem."
 3. "The coffee machine is broken."
 2. "Someone must have put decaf in the wrong pot."
 1. "…In Jesus' name. Amen."

I will bind up the injured and strengthen the weak.

Ezekiel 34:16, NLT

Your spiritual strength comes from God's special favor, not from ceremonial rules.

Hebrews 13:9, NLT

I do not pray for a lighter load, but for a stronger back.

Phillip Brooks[1]

Never try to get out of a dark place except in God's timing and in His way.... Premature delivery may circumvent God's work of grace in your life. Commit the entire situation to Him, and be willing to abide in darkness, knowing He is present. Remember, it is better to walk in the dark with God, than to walk alone in the light.

Stephen Merritt[2]

CHAPTER 10
Bickers and Blunders

*O*ut of the overflow of the heart the mouth speaks.

Matthew 12:34

Do you ever look at your life and wonder, *Did God choose the wrong gal for this job?* I do. Sometimes I survey a day's wreckage—when all the usual household demands, plus a few extra, have sapped my energy so that I feel like a power outlet with ten-too-many extension cords plugged into it—and I'm certain I don't have the personality for this assignment.

The socket shorted out one afternoon when Jessie and Ben got into an argument while I was calmly trying to fix dinner. I started sizzling right along with the ground beef in the pan. Sloppy Joes seemed appropriate, given the sloppy exchange of words around me. I tried to not let their crossfire get the best of me. But...oh, well.

"Hold it!" I ordered with the arresting authority of a SWAT team commander. "Both of you, go to your rooms! I'm not listening to one more word!"

Few things drain me faster than sibling conflict. Even though I'm not the target of their rapid fire, it often feels as if their bullets ricochet around in my stomach, leaving everything inside me torn and ragged.

I know all the clinical stuff. I'm a therapist. I know that sibling rivalry is a normal part of growing up. When you put multiple personalities in an enclosed space, sooner or later sparks fly and combustion results. Kids learn to work with their emotions and deal with their differences through sibling squabbles. Conflict is to be expected, and it can often lead to healthy problem solving and growth. I'm quite familiar with the logic.

But on this particular day, at this particular time, my logic (not to mention my tolerance) was worn thin. Their petty bickering was grating on my ears and my spirit.

Personality plays a part. I'm surrounded by externalizers who are open and vocal when something bothers them. Being an internalizer, I tend to pull in and get quiet. They release their tension and energy. I contain mine. To be sure, there are times when I wish they'd do more containing, and they wish I'd do more releasing.

The impact hits me harder when I'm tired and my defenses are weak. Then those wily little thoughts sneak up on me and whisper, *These things don't happen in healthy families.* Fortunately I know that statement is so absurd that I have to laugh. The truth is that healthy families are not conflict free. The distinguishing mark of a healthy, happy family is that it deals with conflict openly and constructively, rather than with denial, repression, or unlimited expression.

When I shared my frustration with my mentor, she settled into a comfortable position in her chair, took a sip of her coffee, and told me a story of a family she had followed for two generations. She had counseled the mother in earlier years, and later, when she was middle-aged, she counseled the daughter, Lisa. "Lisa grew up in a home where conflict was completely forbidden. The mother worked overtime to keep squabbles from erupting. If a spat did break out, the children were severely punished. They learned at an early age to shove their conflicts underground.

"Lisa's parents meant well. They were good, churchgoing folk who tried to 'keep the peace,' but that peace came at a tremendously high price. After Lisa married and had children of her own, she began to cave in emotionally. She was, sad to say, ill equipped to deal with everyday life and relational problems. Because conflict was never allowed to surface in her growing-up years, she had never learned conflict-management skills.

"So," my mentor told me in summary, "you are giving your children a gift by allowing them some room to fight."

"Oh, I don't mind giving them room," I said with a chuckle,

"but it will be a different room than the one I'm occupying!"

During the next few days, I thought about conflict—and spent some more time refereeing it. Somewhere between officiating sparring matches and other necessary duties of the day, I came across a verse that shed some light on the subject: "May the Lord make your love increase and overflow for each other" (1 Thessalonians 3:12).

As I read the verse several times, I saw that it emphasized *God's* ability to increase our capacity to love to such an extent that it actually overflows. I wondered, *Could this be a truth that stands...*

regardless of opposing points of view?
regardless of differences in personality style?
regardless of early conditioning or environmental shaping?
regardless of the strength or weakness of wills?
regardless of the fact that sometimes our best efforts to manage conflict seem like a futile exercise?

God, I prayed, *I want to see this truth come to pass in our family. As we work out our differences and conflicts, would You, in ways only You can perform, and through circumstances only You can orchestrate, increase our love for one another—in tangible ways that I can see? Would You create such an increase in our love for one another that it spills out all over the place?*

When you pray, watch out for answers.

Obviously if I wanted to witness an example of our love

increasing, I needed to see it in a deprived state first. This occurred one afternoon when we had company for dinner, and I was on the deck, basting salmon on the grill. I heard raised voices in the kitchen. Sure enough—conflict was brewing. John had said something that embarrassed Jessie, and she, being a normal teenager, was venting her frustration. What's worse, this was happening while everyone was milling around the kitchen, waiting for the meat to come off the grill.

Jessie left the kitchen, wiping tears from her eyes. John followed, hoping to make amends. They both felt awful. The rest of us awkwardly tried to defuse the tension the best we could, not really knowing what to say next. It was not a Kodak moment!

I asked for some help filling the glasses with ice and prayed, *Okay, Lord. This is one of those times when we need an overflow of Your love.*

As it turned out, some good things happened that day. John apologized for being insensitive and asked for Jessie's forgiveness. She recovered, washed her face, and put on a smile. Ten minutes later they joined us in the kitchen. John acknowledged his blunder to our guests, they nodded knowingly, and we enjoyed a friendly and lighthearted dinner.

John learned more about sensitivity and being careful with his word choice. Talking to a teen is tricky business. Jessie learned about giving grace and forgiveness. She's going to get to practice this lesson a lot, given that her parents are far from perfect. And our family learned humility. Nothing purges the pride out of you like having company in the front row for a family feud.

And I learned a bit more about God's faithfulness to answer prayer. He heard my whispered plea at the kitchen sink and released the floodgates of His love. The evidence was obvious in the interactions I witnessed over a grilled-salmon dinner. Right smack in the middle of an embarrassing conflict, God did what He does best.

I have to conclude, then, that even if I feel too short for the tall job of loving my family well, God is more than up to the task. Hooray!

Power Perks: A Sip of Hope and Humor

After putting her children to bed, a mother changed into old slacks and a droopy blouse and proceeded to wash her hair. As she heard the children getting more and more rambunctious, her patience grew thin. At last she threw a towel around her head and stormed into their room, putting them back to bed with stern warnings. As she left the room, she heard her three-year-old say with a trembling voice, "Who was that?"

Whatever we have achieved in character, we have achieved through conflict.

J. Wallace Hamilton[1]

We all agree that forgiveness is a beautiful idea until we have to practice it.

C. S. Lewis[2]

If God wants you to do something, He'll make it possible for you to do it, but the grace He provides comes only with the task and cannot be stockpiled beforehand. We are dependent on Him from hour to hour, and the greater our awareness of this fact, the less likely we are to faint or fail in crisis.

Louis Cassels[3]

Be humble and gentle. Be patient with each other, making allowance for each other's faults because of your love. Always keep yourselves united in the Holy Spirit, and bind yourselves together with peace.

Ephesians 4:2–3, NLT

CHAPTER 11

A Longing for Something More

*W*hether you turn to the right or to the left, your ears will hear a voice behind you; saying, "This is the way, walk in it."

Isaiah 30:21

Gretchen gripped the map tightly in her hand, squinting to read the street sign a block ahead of her. While her mother dug through her purse for the rental car keys, Gretchen pondered aloud, "Did we park near the Tomb of the Unknown Soldier?" Her eyes darted back and forth, looking for something familiar. Nothing. She had never been in Philadelphia. It was getting dark, most of the shops were closing, and she and her mother had decided it was time to head back to her brother's home.

It was an eerie feeling. She didn't know if they were in a part of town that was safe at night. The women picked up their pace.

Gretchen's heart raced. She didn't want to upset her mother, so she tried to seem unconcerned. But inside she was silently wondering, *Where on earth are we?*

Several intersections later they spotted the shop where they had purchased cashews earlier that day. With a sigh of relief, they retraced their steps and finally found the car.

As Gretchen drove onto the New Jersey turnpike, she considered the events of the day and got stuck in the moments when she thought they were lost. The feelings were so familiar: The uneasiness. The questioning. The fear. The restless agitation. The exhaustion that comes from perpetually wondering, *Where in the world am I?*

It's a question most women ask, and it's a spiritual rather than geographical one. We want to know where we fit into the divine order of things. We want to understand our destiny. Until we have some answers, the question knocks relentlessly on our door.

"I keep feeling that there is something more—that something is missing from my life, but I'm not sure what," Gretchen reflected in my office. "It's this gnawing feeling that there is a path I'm supposed to be on, but I'm not sure what it is."

The emptiness was overwhelming at times. For years she had written in her journal, attempting to express her deep frustration. The feeling was like an incessant wind. It didn't keep her from living her life, but she wasn't out flying a kite either.

This persistent longing first emerged when Gretchen was in

her early twenties, before she was married. She secretly hoped it would disappear once she walked the aisle. She and her husband had met in high school, dated through college, and married just before starting their careers. They were, and continued to be, best friends. Yet she suffered terrible guilt several months after their ceremony when the unwelcome feelings returned. She asked herself, *How can I feel this way after marrying such a wonderful man? We have a carefree life, great jobs, a comfortable home, and the opportunity for plenty of travel. What is wrong with me?*

Though she tried her best to ignore the nagging emptiness, it continued. She had plenty of diversions and sought fulfillment in each one. Her job at the law firm kept her busy. She loved her work and pursued it with gusto. She also attended seminars, read avidly, and joined associations. In her spare time she aggressively pursued several hobbies. She attended classes, purchased supplies, and ordered books to develop new interests and skills, convinced that her quest would somehow fill the hole in her soul. Though she discovered a natural flair for interior design, her heart remained downtrodden and troubled.

After several years of marriage, Gretchen and her husband decided it was time to start a family. Although the search for "something more" was not her motivation for having children, she did hope the feeling might melt away in the glow of childbirth and mothering. She had already concluded that the emptiness was unrelated to her marriage, her job, or a lack of hobbies.

Not many options remained. Certainly children would bring an added dimension of fulfillment to her life. Having grown up in a close-knit family, she was eager to become a mother.

Gretchen gave birth to a beautiful son and found she enjoyed motherhood even more than she had anticipated. Taking care of her little boy brought tremendous fulfillment, yet again a certain emptiness returned. A couple of years later, Gretchen's daughter was born. One evening, when she was rocking her little one to sleep, Gretchen mused over her questions and concluded, *Maybe nothing is missing. Maybe answers don't exist. I guess I just need to learn to live with these feelings.*

That's when anger took root.

Anyone who looked at Gretchen's life would have concluded she had it all: an attractive and attentive husband, two children she dearly loved, a stimulating career, good health, beauty, bucks, brains. What more could anyone want? Gretchen didn't know. There were many nights when she cried herself to sleep, asking, *Why am I doing this to myself? What does this craving in my soul mean?*

Understand that Gretchen did have a relationship with God. But she felt that since He had already blessed her with more than her fair share, it seemed ungrateful to pray about her restlessness. She didn't discuss these matters with her friends because they had enough struggles of their own. And she kept the issues out of her family life. She tried alone, for years, to bury the feelings that made her feel half alive.

Finally she could live with the dissatisfaction no longer. She made an appointment and entered my office ready to work. As I listened to her articulate explanation, I asked the Lord for wisdom in assessing her needs. After hearing her story, I said, "Gretchen, it seems to me that you are at an exciting juncture."

She looked puzzled.

I continued, "You have told me that you feel like there is more out there for you. You have a sense that something is missing, even though you have no apparent conflicts in your relationships or in the roles you fill. In every sense of the word, life is good, except for this vague feeling of emptiness."

"Yes, that's right," she answered.

"Could it be that God is trying to get your attention through these feelings of discontent?" I asked. "Have you asked God how He might want to use you to make a difference in this world?"

She sat quietly for a moment. "No," she answered, "I don't believe I ever have."

I shared a significant statement I read in college that had stuck with me. A. H. Maslow, an existential psychologist, wrote: "All human beings must seek their God-given mission in their lifetime." He proposed this idea simply as a basic principle of good mental health, but his idea parallels what the Bible teaches: God has a specific plan for each of us.

Some women are resigned to the belief that the events of life are basically random in nature, a sort of roll of the cosmic dice.

That wasn't Gretchen's view. She believed in God. She believed He loved her and that He accompanied her through life on a daily basis. She was grateful for the gifts and talents with which He had blessed her. She had just never made the connection that He might desire to use her for His purposes, or that there might be a specific plan He would have for her.

She was doing her best to be a good steward of what God had given her. Based on her natural talents and interests, she had conscientiously mapped out her agenda. She strove for excellence and authenticity in all she did. But she had not sought God and *His* agenda or discovered what He had in mind when He made her. I explained that whatever plan God had for Gretchen would incorporate the gifts He had given her and that His assignments would bring far more fulfillment and meaning than she could experience through her own efforts.

I remember the moment of enlightenment and the "Ah-ha!" experience I had when I discovered this truth for myself. Like Gretchen, I was in my early twenties when, as I pondered these issues, Paul's words became meaningful to me: "For we are God's workmanship, created in Christ Jesus to do good works, which God prepared in advance for us to do" (Ephesians 2:10) and "It is God who works in you to will and to act according to his good purpose" (Philippians 2:13).

It's my conviction that if we, as women, are to lead deep, rich, fulfilling lives, we need to be open and responsive to God.

We need to ask on a daily basis, *Lord, how do You want to use me today, in my little corner of the world, with the gifts and talents You've given me? Please show me how I can participate in Your purposes, and carry out the good works You have planned for me to do.*

When Gretchen came to my office the following week, we picked up where we had left off. It became obvious to me that the Spirit of God had been at work, and she had more answers than she knew what to do with.

On Sunday she and her husband had attended church as usual. On that particular Sunday, it was as if her pastor had read her private journal, even her thoughts. In his message he told the congregation that God wanted each of them to make a difference in this world. She sat in her seat with tears welling in her eyes, excited to realize that the Lord was speaking to her.

As the week wore on, the idea of finding her God-given mission seemed to bombard her from every direction. A friend called to talk, and in a roundabout way, she challenged Gretchen to think about what God might want to do with her life. When Gretchen was reading her Bible, she collided head-on with a verse that drove the point home again. Paul said: "I keep going on, *trying to grasp that purpose* for which Christ Jesus grasped me" (Philippians 3:12, PHP, emphasis mine).

Gretchen met with her pastor to tell him about her recent revelations. He assured her that God would reveal His plan as she listened carefully and patiently for His answers. She positioned herself and waited. Then God began showing her things about herself she had never seen before. She began to sense a passionate desire to help other women. She was bursting with ideas. The church she attended didn't have a women's program, so she returned to her pastor's office to discuss the possibilities. He had been praying for a long time that someone would accept the challenge of coordinating a ministry for women.

And that was all the confirmation Gretchen needed.

A year later, Gretchen was facilitating women's retreats and leading a Sunday morning Bible study. She had never done anything like that before, but if you were to see her in action, you would think she was an old pro. And she is brimming with the fulfillment of knowing her place, as designed by God, in the world.

She's moved from asking God to bless what she does to asking God what He wants her to do—and assuming that that's where His blessing resides. It's an approach she uses at home as a wife and mother, on the job at the law firm, and wherever else she is involved.

You, too, can experience the fullness of God's perfect plan for you. Did you know He made you specifically, with unique tasks that only you can accomplish? Did you know He constructed a map just for you, so you would never feel lost?

Ask Him.

Power Perks: A Sip of Hope and Humor

An elderly couple was sitting on their porch swing, rocking away the stresses of the day while watching the sunset. They interrupted the silence now and then with comments about the "good old days."

Grandma turned to Grandpa and said, "Honey, do you remember how, when we first started dating, you used to casually reach over and take my hand?"

Grandpa looked at her, smiled, and obligingly took her hand in his.

With a wry little grin, Grandma pressed a little farther. "Honey, do you remember how, when we were courting, you used to lean over and suddenly kiss me on the cheek?"

Grandpa leaned toward Grandma and gave her a lingering kiss on her soft, wrinkled cheek.

With added boldness, Grandma said, "Honey, do you remember how, after we were married, you kind of nibbled on my ear?"

Grandpa slowly got up from the porch swing and shuffled his way to the front door.

Alarmed, Grandma said, "Honey, where are you going?"

"To get my teeth!"

Men are from earth. Women are from earth. Deal with it.

George Carlin

The average life span of a woman is constantly increasing, thus enabling her to stay 29 much longer.[1]

God always gives His very best to those who leave the choice with Him.

Hudson Taylor[2]

God's gifts put man's best dreams to shame.

Elizabeth Browning[3]

CHAPTER 12

Bugs in the Brew

Whatever you do, work at it with all your heart, as working for the Lord, not for men, since you know that you will receive an inheritance from the Lord as a reward. It is the Lord Christ you are serving.

Colossians 3:23–24

Cynthia's question caught me completely off guard. After rattling off a long list of nasty comments a family member had made about her, she paused, took a deep breath, and asked, "How do *you* deal with people who put you down?"

"Well, I guess it depends on the circumstances," I responded.

"How about this? I recently showed a lady your book, *Angel Behind the Rocking Chair.* When I started telling her about one of my favorite chapters, she interrupted me with a smirk and shook her head in disdain, saying: 'I don't know why Pam would write a book about children with special needs. She's no expert.'"

Somewhat stunned, I wondered how to graciously catch this curveball. As I sipped my coffee, I could tell from Cynthia's voice and penetrating look that she really wanted an answer.

Her question went beyond a general interest in how I would handle this situation. She was trying to glean some insight into dealing with her own set of struggles. For years she had endured the toxic taunts of a critical mother and a perfectionistic twin sister. No matter what she did, in their eyes, it was never good enough. It didn't matter if she knocked herself out for her husband. It didn't matter if she was "mother of the year" to her kids. She was constantly advised on ways she could do better. Having endured years of perpetual put-downs, she wanted some suggestions to take home with her after we emptied the coffeepot.

You need to know something else about Cynthia. She is a Geiger counter for phoniness. She has no patience for platitudes, and she seeks truth earnestly, swatting away any superficiality as she would a mosquito.

Swallowing another sip of coffee, I said, "Well, comments like those never feel good. I'd prefer to hear that people enjoy reading my books." But her question triggered a memory that I decided to share with her. I reached for my prayer journal and told the story.

One day, years ago, someone's sharp words had sliced me to

shreds. The remarks had been cloaked in spiritual jargon to make them sound like "constructive criticism." But there was nothing remotely useful or helpful about them. They were vague, sweeping generalizations that masqueraded as facts. To put it plain and simple, I was royally reamed.

My response? At the time I said nothing, but I admit I didn't do a good job of shaking it off. That pitiful one-minute interaction gnawed at me for days, like an old dog working over his favorite bone. It chewed on me, put me aside, then chewed on me some more. It's amazing how, if we let it, one negative remark can nullify one hundred positive comments.

Those ugly, nagging words drove me to my Father for comfort and insight. I told Cynthia how after three days of ruminating, I decided I had replayed the incident too often. I tucked the kids in bed, prayed with them, and then curled up in a comfortable chair with my Bible and prayer journal, still bugged. And I was even bugged that I was bugged. I didn't like the fact that someone's barbs had successfully ripped the rug out from under my confidence and sent my sense of contentment crashing into a million and one pieces.

So I prayed. I asked God for wisdom, and I considered the event again. I wrote my conclusions in my prayer journal:

Lord, every good gift in my life is from You. My husband. My children. My writing. My speaking. My counseling. It's all yours. And the bottom line is that it is You, and You alone, I want to please. I want to live my life [for] an audience of One.

There will come a day when I will render a final account to You for what I've done in this life.

I won't stand before You and be asked to give an account for my husband's life.

I won't stand before You and be asked to give an account for my children's lives.

I won't stand before You and be asked to give an account for my friends' lives…or my critics' words.

On the day I see You face-to-face, You will look me in the eye and ask *me* about *me*. Period.

That night I asked myself: *Do you feel you have done what God wanted you to do?* I could honestly answer yes. And I realized that was all that really mattered.

Cynthia pondered what I said. I closed my journal, reached for my coffee cup, and thought about the peace those perspectives had delivered to my troubled heart years ago. "Ahhhh," Cynthia said, sipping the last few drops from her mug. "If I'm doing my best for God, then that is good enough."

"Yes!" I said, excited that the point had hit home. "That's the very place where freedom from disapproval begins."

Sometime after that conversation, I looked up a passage of Scripture I had read many times before. The apostle Paul, who frequently endured the heat from every Tom, Dick, and Harry who offered a critical review of his life, asked himself a question similar to the one in my journal: "Am I now trying to win the approval of men, or of God? Or am I trying to please men? If I were still trying to please men, I would not be a servant of Christ" (Galatians 1:10).

Once again the perfect simplicity of Paul's words inspired me. Pleasing man and serving God are, at times, mutually exclusive. When we give our lives wholeheartedly to follow God's plan for our lives, there will be people who won't be pleased with us. There will be those who won't like what we do or how we do it. They won't like what we say or how we look. They'll have strong opinions about what we should or shouldn't be doing.

There will be judgment.

There will be confrontations.

There will be put-downs.

And when those painful times come, we must be careful to respond in ways that please the Lord. We must not get hooked into petty snarls. We must monitor our responses and let God be the One to set the record straight.

Paul also wrote, "Each of us will give an account of himself to God. Therefore let us stop passing judgment on one another. Instead, *make up your mind* not to put any stumbling block or obstacle in your brother's way" (Romans 14:12–13, emphasis mine).

Hmm. That sounds like a choice to me. It also sounds like a

challenge—a challenge to mind my own business and to be about His business. It's what pleases Him and liberates you and me.

I've noticed something. The more I remind myself of the promise of God's favor and grace, the less I feel the need to defend myself when critics open fire. Living my life for an audience of One has the power to turn down the heat on hurtful hints so my emotions don't boil over and burn others.

The next time you're stung by a barb or pierced by a swiftly flying arrow, remember there is only One you need to please. Align yourself with Him, step behind the wide shield of faith, and leave your defense in His capable hands. He knows best how to handle the nasty bugs that land in your brew.

Power Perks: A Sip of Hope and Humor

Sitting on the side of the highway waiting to catch speeding drivers, a state trooper saw a car puttering along at twenty-two miles per hour. He thought, *This driver is just as dangerous as a speeder!* So he turned on his lights and pulled the driver over.

Approaching the car, he noticed that there were five old ladies—two in the front seat and three in the back—wide-eyed and white as ghosts. The driver, obviously confused, said to him, "Officer, I don't understand, I was doing exactly the speed limit! What seems to be the problem?"

"Ma'am," the officer replied, "you weren't speeding, but you should know that driving slower than the speed limit can also be a danger to other drivers."°

"Slower than the speed limit? No, sir, I was doing the speed limit exactly—twenty-two miles an hour!" the old woman said a bit proudly.

The state trooper, trying to contain a chuckle, explained to her that twenty-two was the route number, not the speed limit.

A bit embarrassed, the woman grinned and thanked the officer for pointing out her error.

"But before I let you go, ma'am, I have to ask—is everyone in this car okay? These women seem awfully shaken, and they haven't uttered a single peep this whole time," the officer said.

"Oh, they'll be all right in a minute, officer. We just got off Route 119."

A cynic is a man who, when he smells the flowers, looks around for a coffin.

H. L. Mencken[1]

—∞—

I cannot control the cruel things said by others; but living my life for an audience of One can help me disregard them.

—∞—

He who seeks only for applause from without has all his happiness in another's keeping.[2]

—∞—

What you don't see with your eyes, don't invent with your mouth.
Jewish Proverb[3]

CHAPTER 13

Shaped for a Higher Purpose

An instrument for noble purposes...
made holy, useful to the Master and prepared to do any good work.

2 Timothy 2:21

Since *Angel Behind the Rocking Chair* was published, I have received cards and letters from families across the country. I have laughed and cried through the personal stories they have shared with me. Karen from New Jersey told me about her daughter, Patty, who has Down's syndrome. Patty is now six years old, and Karen and her husband joke that God must have installed an Energizer battery in her. This little spitfire goes from sunup until sundown and never runs out of gas. Like our little Nathan, Patty is as quick as lightning and a professional escape artist. Her parents say, tongue in cheek, that her extra chromosome is packed full of stubbornness.

Boy, did that ring a bell! I've noticed the same thing about Nathan. He's an interesting mix of tough and tender. He's strong-willed and sensitive, forceful and fragile. One minute he's the happiest, most affectionate little guy on earth. The next he's throwing a fit, demanding what he wants, unwilling to bend to behavioral interventions that are "supposed" to work.

Unfortunately, I recognize the same traits in myself. I wish I could say that I always respond quickly to God in cheerful compliance. I wish I could say that I always trust Him—that I never argue, talk back, or demand my own way. Sometimes the very things I wish my own children wouldn't do, I find myself doing with God.

I remember one night when I was rocking Nathan to sleep. My soul was as dark as the night. Nathan was approaching his sixth birthday, and birthdays seem to trigger both joy and grief even when I try to focus on celebration. We have so much for which to be thankful. But on this particular night I must have been especially worn out because my "attitude of gratitude" had flown the coop. I was in the middle of a power struggle with God.

I didn't want Nathan to be mentally retarded. I wanted him to be "normal."

I didn't want Nathan to be mute. I longed to hear his thoughts and feelings.

I didn't want Nathan to need special assistance at school and church. I wanted him to be independent and capable like Jessie and Ben.

I didn't want to change one more diaper! Six years was enough.

I had been in this place before, struggling with the discrepancy between the ideal and the real. *How*, I wondered, *am I going to plan a fun-filled birthday party for Nathan while I'm in the middle of throwing myself a first-class pity party?* Tears fell, and I rocked Nathan for a long time that evening—more for my sake than his.

During those quiet moments, an unexpected insight came. I sensed God saying, "Pam, I always give you My best." The truth penetrated the core of my soul. I wept. God had shined a spotlight on my prideful stubborn will.

I wanted what I wanted, when I wanted it. And I wasn't happy because I hadn't gotten my way. Looking back, I think I honestly believed that I knew what was best for Nathan and the rest of us, and it didn't include a diagnosis of Down's syndrome.

I've seen other women struggle to accept difficult, harsh realities in life....

Debby, whose husband decided he didn't want to be married to her any longer and left town with a younger woman.

Trish, whose daughter was declared legally blind just after her first birthday.

Miriam, who was passed up for a promotion because she didn't play office politics.

Kathryn, who has spent years battling cancer.

Diane, who hasn't heard from her son in more than ten years.

Mary, who lost her beloved husband to a heart attack at the relatively young age of forty-two.

For all of us, whatever our circumstance, the realization that "this is not what I want" triggers grief. But no one always gets what she wants. And when we realize this, we have a choice. We can act like petulant children. We can argue, resist, slam doors, demand our way, and pout. Or we can rightfully grieve and then surrender to the Lord our God and focus our belief on His bigger, more perfect plan. We can clench our fists and shake them in angry defiance, or we can open our hands in acceptance and ask God to take what we yield to Him and give us His best.

A passage in the book of Jeremiah spoke candidly to me about my self-will:

> The LORD gave another message to Jeremiah. He said, "Go down to the shop where clay pots and jars are made. I will speak to you while you are there." So I did as he told me and found the potter working at his wheel. But the jar he was making did not turn out as he had hoped, so the potter squashed the jar into a lump of clay and started again.

> Then the LORD gave me this message: "Can I not
> do to you as this potter has done to his clay? As the clay
> is in the potter's hand, so are you in my hand."
> (Jeremiah 18:1–6, NLT)

When I read that passage, I realized that my resistance to the fact that Nathan was handicapped caused much of my anguish. Have you ever noticed that resisting circumstances does not change things? What is, is. Wrestling with reality gets us nowhere. But the prophet grants us perspective. We are in the Potter's hands. We can trust that no matter where we are at this particular time in our lives, God wants to give us His best. Recognizing our resistance is the first step to moving beyond it. It can propel us toward acceptance, if we let it. Knowing the difference between a problem to be solved and a fact to be accepted is crucial to our peace of mind.

When I'm more objective, I can see that much of my resistance comes from fear. *And fear is an enemy that cannot be trusted.* It blinds me to the fact that God is all-sufficient and that He will take care of me, no matter what comes my way.

Hard things happen in this world. We pray. We wait. We listen. We talk. And even then sometimes things are still fuzzy and hard to understand. No one warned us that this particular phase of the journey would be this dark. This rocky. This steep. This crushing.

Yet as we dwell in the Potter's hands, even though we may be in pain, confused, and conflicted, we can trust that God is in the middle of shaping us. For what? For what Paul called His "noble purposes." In pure faith we can rest, knowing His intentions are good. His movement is precise. His direction is strategic. We are being changed. Healed. Reconstructed and transformed into His image. He's working. He's shaping. He's molding. He's removing impurities and refining us like gold. It's our job to be pliable in His strong and tender hands.

We can trust that God cares about that which we hold dear to our hearts. In time more clarity will come. He really can make all things work together for our best—even the strange, unplanned situations that seem to blindside us. We can trust that in the years ahead, we will look back on today's issues and see how God used them to shape us into a vessel worthy of honor. Even our worst mistakes can become springboards that launch us into divine assignments.

That dark night as I sat rocking Nathan, my divine assignment was to make a holy exchange: my grief and my demands for God's assurance that the Potter was at work. I needed to become less childish and more childlike—like Nathan, relaxed, sleeping soundly in his parent's arms, confident that all was well. I needed to remember that God is a master Artist, and that He makes only masterpieces.

Power Perks: A Sip of Hope and Humor

You know you're a victim of Worn-Out Woman Syndrome when…

- You wonder if brewing is really a necessary step for the consumption of coffee.
- You ask the drive-through attendant at your favorite Espresso Express if you can get your double mocha to go.
- Apart from coffee, tropical-flavored Tums become your sole source of sustenance.
- Your family finds you in a fetal position on the kitchen floor after you discovered that the timer on your coffeemaker didn't work.
- You keep yelling, "Leave me alone!" even though no one else is anywhere near you.

THE TOP TEN THINGS MEN UNDERSTAND ABOUT WOMEN

10.

9.

8.

7.

6.

5.

4.

3.

2.

1.

Faith means being grasped by a power that is greater than we are, a power that shakes us and turns us, and transforms and heals us. Surrender to this power is faith.

Paul Tillich[1]

Pride is spiritual cancer; it eats the very possibility of love or contentment, or even common sense.

C. S. Lewis[2]

Live near to God so all things will appear to you little in comparison with eternal realities.

Robert McCheyne[3]

If your first concern is to look after yourself, you'll never find yourself. But if you forget about yourself and look to me, you'll find both yourself and me.

Matthew 10:39, MSG

CHAPTER 14

When You Are at Wit's End Corner

hey were at their wits' end.
Then they cried out to the LORD in their trouble,
and he brought them out of their distress.

Psalm 107:27–28

Suicide. The ultimate resignation. The final waving of the white flag. The seeming end to frustration and failure—except for those left behind.

Judy knew her husband of thirty-one years was in pain. Bart was a talented and gifted man, accomplished in his profession and the recipient of many accolades for outstanding performances. Letters and plaques lined his walls, documenting his superb leadership abilities. Yet his highly successful career came to a crashing halt when his company downsized. Disappointment merged with fear as Bart applied for a new job and saw it awarded to a younger man. Complicating his first taste of unemployment was a long-denied and untreated depression. When he did find a new position, his illness had taken such a hold that he was unable to function. As the months passed, Judy watched her strong, steady husband buckle to his knees.

Six weeks after he started his new position, Bart attempted suicide. Medical teams intervened and ushered him into follow-up treatment for depression. With the help of medication, therapy, and prayer, Bart seemed to improve. The couple relocated, and he accepted a job with fewer demands.

A few months later, however, the symptoms returned. Bart admitted that the specter of suicide was haunting him. Judy took him to a new doctor, and they tried many new medications. But Judy was concerned about the process—the doctor seemed to change drugs abruptly, and he didn't seem to delve very thoroughly into Bart's problem. Worse, every medication brought severe side effects that only deepened his despair. After fourteen months of a vicious battle, Bart chose not to fight anymore, and he killed himself. In a letter he left behind, he said that he believed he was doing what was best.

At Bart's funeral, the pastor's words were balm to Judy in the midst of her shattering grief: "Our friend died on his own battlefield. He was killed in action fighting a civil war. He fought against adversaries that were as real to him as his casket is to us. They were powerful adversaries. They took a toll on his energies and endurance. They exhausted the last vestiges of his courage, and only God knows how this child of His suffered in the silent skirmishes that took place in his soul."

Still Judy found herself engulfed in a sea of self-recrimination. Intrusive thoughts bombarded her mind: *If only you had been a better wife...more sensitive...more supportive...more tuned in to his needs...more assertive with the doctor...this never would have happened.* Those were the inside conflicts. The outside problems were every bit as real.

Judy needed money to survive, but every occupational door she approached slammed in her face. She had so many rejection notices she could have papered a wall. Horrific panic attacks swept over her before interviews—there were times she had to retreat to her car to regain composure. Finally, feeling hopelessly trapped, she constructed a plan to terminate her own pain. All the odds seemed to be stacked against her. Life had wedged her into a no-win situation. In her own words, "I had waited so long for God to answer my prayer for peace, that it was just too painful to hope any longer." Or so she thought.

That's how it is for most of us. When we're worn down by unrelenting conflicts from without and within, it's very easy to draw the conclusion that this is how life will *always* be. When our defenses are weakened, we tend to forecast negatively into the future. Our minds become overly active, flashing worst-case scenarios before our eyes. But there is a basic law of nature that applies to all of us: *Nothing lasts forever, this side of heaven.* An unusual set of circumstances drove that truth deep into Judy's heart.

One Wednesday night, Judy pulled herself together to go to church. She doesn't recall what the pastor talked about, but she does remember how he paused at the end of his sermon, looked her direction, and said, "There is a woman here tonight who is struggling with the will to live. The Lord wants you to know that He loves you."

God had her attention.

The following Sunday Judy went back to church, and much to her astonishment the same scenario occurred. The pastor paused after his message and said, "There is a woman here today who is contemplating suicide. God has a message for you. Hang in there. Better days are ahead for you."

In all the years Judy had attended that church, she had never seen the pastor do that. Later that day, in the privacy of her home she responded to the Lord: *Okay, God, if You love me enough to single me out of four thousand people to give me that message twice, I surrender. If You can make something out of this pile of manure in my life—go for it. It's Yours. Every last bit of it.*

Even though her prayer was a bit brassy, it proved to be pivotal. With Christmas around the bend, Judy found a seasonal position as a sales associate at a department store. The job was a welcome answer to prayer, but the part-time hours assigned her would not bring in enough income to cover her bills. Her savings had dwindled to zero. She had no money to pay her property taxes. Her car insurance was due January first, and she had not purchased a single Christmas present for her family.

One morning before work, Judy sat on the edge of her bed, flipping through her checkbook, rehearsing a laundry list of unmet needs. *Lord, I don't have a husband anymore to pay the bills. You're the only One I can depend on to provide for me. But frankly, Lord, it doesn't look like You are doing Your part! I need help—at least five hundred dollars to stay afloat, and many more hours at work. Lord, would You please have someone from my family call to check on me?*

She left for her job, trying to muster the courage to request more hours. But when she arrived, she discovered that her supervisor was one step ahead. Judy was on the books for forty hours a week for the next five weeks.

That night Judy kicked off her shoes after a long day at work, surprised that God had answered her prayer so quickly. But she was even more amazed a few minutes later when the phone rang, and one of her sisters was on the other end of the line. The call itself wasn't an unusual occurrence. The gals talked frequently. But what her sister said at the end of the conversation almost knocked Judy off her tired feet: "Judy, I don't know how to say this, but I guess I'll just ask. Could you by any chance use five hundred dollars?"

Stunned, Judy didn't know whether to laugh or cry. How did

her sister know? Who had given her the inside scoop? What prompted her to make such an offer on the very day Judy had prayed for specific help? The answer was clear. Only God could have done that.

Two months later Judy received another surprise phone call. It was her father saying that he wanted to pay her property taxes. She hadn't asked him for help. But the Spirit of God knew every detail of Judy's suffering, and as only He can do, He prompted her dad to step in and help.

The provisions have continued, day after day, month after month, and year after year. Today, Judy's bills are paid in full. She has savings in the bank. Her health is stronger. Her job is the passion of her life. And her healing influence on the lives of other men and women is dramatic.

Wit's End Corner, you see, is not a dead end.

It is an intersection.

When you are suffering unimaginable pain, very suddenly you find yourself at a point of decision. You can hang out at the Corner, stymied by pain. You can retreat, as Bart did, taking a final exit. Or you can take a step onto a new road and find your circumstances moving in a different direction. Your perspective is altered. You see life from a new angle. Your situation becomes clearer, as if you just put on an improved pair of glasses. Life is more manageable. Tiny rays of light begin to point your way out of the dark.

For some it happens sooner than later. For most, the changes that we long for don't happen nearly as fast as we'd like. But there are likely divine purposes at work behind those delays. And while we're waiting, there is something we can do that will release hope in our hearts.

We can *believe*. Not in fate. Not in the power of positive thinking. Not in some nebulous goodwill that floats around the universe. We can believe in the Lord our God, who is the Cornerstone of life itself.

A believing heart cries out from beneath insurmountable burdens and says, *God, I don't understand any of this. And frankly, I'd prefer anything to this suffering. But…*

- *I believe that somehow You will use these unparalleled difficulties for my good.*
- *I believe that You are bigger and greater and stronger than any of my circumstances.*
- *I believe that You will fulfill your purposes in me, no matter what.*
- *I believe that even if everyone else breaks his promise, You will be faithful. You will turn things around.*
- *I believe that even if nothing changes on the outside, You will change me on the inside and give me what I need to be able to go on.*

Jesus said, "If you believe, then you will see" (John 11:40). Judy believed, and she has seen. She has rounded the curve and passed from Wit's End Corner to Prosperity Drive. Those who know Judy today find it hard to imagine that she was ever broken, weary, or groping in the dark. Now she stands straight and tall. Her countenance radiates peace. Her words carry the penetrating power of one who has tasted death and resurrection life. As a member of a church staff that serves more than seven thousand people, Judy touches hearts with a message of God's healing grace, a truth her husband was never able to grasp.

What about you? What are you facing? Has a new set of problems appeared on the horizon, leaving you troubled about today and fearful about tomorrow?

Are you fatigued and battle-worn by a long string of chronic stresses? Do you wonder when, or if, they will ever end?

Is your nose pressed tight up against the wall at Wit's End Corner while you wait for God's provision?

Friend, God's purposes in your life will not fail to be accomplished. There is no person big enough to derail His plans for you. There is no circumstance, fatigue, depression, or form of suffering that can thwart His agenda. Even when your prayers seem to be bouncing off the ceiling, God is actively orchestrating on your behalf. Rest assured, a breakthrough is on the way. Change is coming.

More than likely, it's just around the corner.

P.S. If you're facing overwhelming circumstances and feeling the pressure of depression—if suicide seems like the best choice—please contact a health-care professional immediately. He or she, and medication, may be able to help you cope more effectively as you wait prayerfully for God's intervention.

Power Perks: A Sip of Hope and Humor

Two ladies were shipwrecked on an island. One lay against a palm tree, calm and serene. The other stood screaming, "We're going to die! There's no food, no water, no shelter! Don't you understand? We're going to die!"

The first lady replied, *"You* don't understand. I make one hundred thousand dollars a week."

The second lady looked dumbfounded. "What difference does that make? We're on an island with no food or water. We're going to die!"

The first lady answered, "You just don't get it. I make one hundred thousand dollars a week and I tithe ten percent to the church. Relax! My pastor will find us!"

If God has made your cup sweet, drink it with grace. If he has made it bitter, drink it in communion with him.

Oswald Chambers[1]

When our faith, hope, and love ends, God's begins.[2]

CHAPTER 15

The Road Taken

And let us not get tired of doing what is right,
for after a while we will reap a harvest of blessing
if we don't get discouraged and give up.

Galatians 6:9, TLB

For those of us who follow Christ, the long road to heaven is often pockmarked with potholes of temptation and speed bumps of bad choices. My friend Tamara knows this firsthand. During one of our afternoon walks around the neighborhood, she bravely shared her story with me. Like dozens I've heard in my counseling office, it underscores the nasty nature of temptation. In the end, its victims are always left lying by the side of the road, bruised and barely breathing.

I'll let Tamara tell her dramatic story.

It all started at a time when my professional life was particularly exciting. I was the vice president of a bank and managed forty-five people. A real perk was the opportunity to travel and attend training and development seminars where I could meet others in my field. One summer I decided to attend a national conference in the financial services industry, designed specifically for African-American professionals. Four hundred people attended, and I felt like a kid in a huge candy store with a dollar to spend.

You see, living in the Pacific Northwest, I was accustomed to being one of few African-Americans who attended these kinds of conferences. I was clearly in the minority. On this occasion, for the first time in my life, I experienced what it was like to be in the majority. It was an emotional high unlike any other.

Those feelings were surging when I met Sam. He arrived at the class late, searched for a place to sit, and found an empty seat next to me. At first glance I realized this guy was one of the most handsome I'd ever seen—a first-class gentleman from New York. Throughout the conference we saw each other from a distance in various workshops, at the social functions, and during free time. Sam was always perfectly kind and treated me with the utmost respect. Not once did he make any improper advances. There were other men who tested the waters with me. I was slow in perceiving their intentions, but when the lights turned on, in a way I found their interest flattering. In another way I found it disgusting. I didn't want to be anyone's object.

When the conference ended, Sam and I exchanged business cards, as I did with at least thirty other professionals. I flew home and resumed life as usual. A few weeks later, though, Sam called, and our secret relationship began. What started out as an occasional chat to "see how things were going" turned into weekly calls during which we discussed everything from professional issues to our dreams, our hopes, our fears, our spouses, and our children.

Yes, I was married. But my marriage was troubled; my husband, Aaron, and I had become enveloped in our careers and were growing apart. We spoke with each other mostly about the children or to exchange schedules. When I attended that fateful conference, I was feeling charged by my career, but unfulfilled in my marriage.

The more Sam and I talked, the tighter our bond grew, and the more I wanted to see him. It wasn't long before the perfect opportunity presented itself. The bank sent me to a conference in Boston. I knew the workshop topics would interest Sam, so I suggested he attend the conference, too. I sent in my registration, made travel arrangements, and eagerly awaited the trip.

A few weeks later Sam called to say that he was unable to make reservations for that weekend because all the hotels in the area were booked solid due to a sports event. Unless a cancellation occurred, he wouldn't be able to make the trip.

Conveniently I had already booked a suite that had two

queen-size beds. I told Sam that he was welcome to use the room. I had some concerns about this, but I rationalized that it would be like sharing a room with one of my brothers. I viewed my relationship with Sam as platonic. He was simply a close friend and professional colleague.

Looking back, I can see how my rationalizations set me up. I thought that because I had a strong relationship with God, an affair could never tempt me. I believed that as long as I didn't have sexual contact, there was no harm in spending time with this other man. At the time I viewed Aaron, not me, as the source of our marriage problems. I had convinced myself that if Aaron were only more supportive, more understanding, and less controlling, I could reach my goals. I figured I had made huge sacrifices and invested years of my life in my husband and children. I remember saying to myself, *Now it is my turn. It's time to pursue my career dreams. I can do it all. I can have it all.*

I went to Boston and shared my room with Sam. As you might expect, the temptation was more than any human being with a pulse could resist. When I returned to Portland after this intimate encounter, our phone calls increased in frequency and length. My heart was hooked, and I found myself rearranging my schedule so that I was always in my office when Sam typically called. At home I spent most of my time with the kids or alone. My emotional tank was well filled by my secret friend.

I'm not sure how Aaron knew, but he sensed something was

up. One night he decided to look through my briefcase. He had never done this before, but his action was rewarded. He found the evidence in the inside pocket: a love letter I had written Sam and planned to mail the next day. My secret was exposed.

It was heart wrenching to witness the crushing blow on Aaron. Even though I was no longer in love with him, I did care about him. Neither of us knew what to do. Aaron's world was falling apart, and while I sympathized, I was still emotionally involved with Sam. I couldn't give him up, yet I knew I was risking everything. We both felt like our hearts were being ripped to shreds.

In spite of all the emotional confusion Aaron was suffering, he remained very clear and focused on his priorities. His wife and his children were his most valued treasures, and he wasn't about to give them up without a fight. I'm sure there were times when he wondered if the pain he was suffering was worth the hassle, but he stuck with it. In the face of my infidelity, he seemed to renew his vows.

The pressure was more than I could take. I decided to rent an apartment so I could have some space in which to sort things out. Aaron reluctantly accepted the idea. I made what I thought was an unselfish decision at that time: I left the children, who were teens, with Aaron. I knew the statistics about the financial impact of divorce, and I figured that if we ended up splitting they would have more advantages with him.

I had lived in that little apartment for about a month when

a call from my aunt jolted me back to reality. This particular aunt has a reputation of being the pious, religious one in the family. When I heard her voice, I fully expected a Bible-thumping, verse-quoting, hellfire-and-damnation lecture. But she simply asked a question: "Tamara, do you really want another woman living in your house with your husband and raising your children?"

The thought had never crossed my mind. For some reason I had always pictured Aaron alone with the kids. Talk about a delusion! There isn't a woman I know who wouldn't consider Aaron a great catch. Shaken to my senses, I saw that once I was out of the picture, other women would set their sights on Aaron, and he would be gone for good. I moved back home.

Yet my connection with Sam continued. For the next several months I continued to rendezvous with him when I traveled East on business. Our sexual involvement was limited to the one occurrence in Boston—physical intimacy was not the driving force in this relationship. Emotional intimacy was. I had transferred my affection from Aaron to Sam; Sam had become my confidante and Aaron an outsider. It was the emotional lifeline Sam seemed to offer that I couldn't give up.

Of course my lifelong faith was in complete conflict with my behavior. The thoughts ran through my mind constantly: *Tamara, what are you doing?* Living in conflict with my beliefs was totally out of character for me. I had never compromised my values before, either professionally or personally. I grew up follow-

ing the rules, getting good grades, walking the straight and narrow, and saying no before marriage. This track record made it
easy for Aaron and my family to believe that I was an innocent
victim who had been seduced by a smooth-talking Casanova. But
I knew that wasn't true. I was as responsible for the relationship
as Sam was.

Between the conflicts that raged between my talk and my
walk, and my living with Aaron while pursuing my relationship
with Sam, I experienced constant turmoil. Naturally, so did
Aaron. We both had difficulty managing the stress. He broke out
in a nasty rash that covered his entire body in welts. I was unable
to eat or sleep and felt like I was about to snap. I overreacted to
minor irritants. I finally realized I needed professional help. In an
effort to preserve the scraps of self-esteem and sanity I had left, I
made an appointment with a therapist.

I was careful to select a therapist without an obvious spiritual
orientation because I didn't want someone to lecture me on right
and wrong. I was well aware of those issues. But I felt trapped. I
didn't want to end my relationship with Sam—or with Aaron.

One of the key elements that therapy brought out was the
way my public life and my personal life were not integrated. I was
not living in sync with my values. I was challenged to ask myself
questions like: *Who am I? What do I believe? Are my beliefs really
mine or my parents? How are these beliefs evident in the various roles
I perform?* Answering those questions honestly, over time, caused

an internal shift. I knew that what I was doing wasn't for anyone's highest good. Lies and betrayal are the devil's IOUs. Weary of the effects of my wrongs and angry for hurting myself and others, I began to make changes—from the inside out.

It eventually became clear to me that I had two options. I could terminate my marriage and continue with Sam. If I did this, I would need to change my belief system to fit the behavior because living one way and believing another was destroying me.

The second option was to terminate my relationship with Sam and work on my marriage. If my beliefs really were mine, this was the only choice that would allow for congruence. So, three years after my initial contact with Sam, I made a conscious decision to replace my excuses with a fresh determination to rebuild my marriage. Ending that friendship was one of the most difficult decisions of my life.

I went to work on my marriage. Aaron and I enrolled in some marriage enrichment classes. While this was an important step in the healing process, I often felt as if I was just going through the motions. My head was in the marriage, but my heart wasn't. I still had an unquenchable yearning to communicate with Sam.

I realized I needed to recover my relationship with God. I had neglected it so much that it almost didn't exist at this point, but I could see that my healing was beyond me. I sought God's forgiveness. I started asking Him to help me reestablish the marital relationship I once had. I asked Him to rekindle the fires of love and passion for Aaron that had been ablaze during our courtship. It was a prayer of faith from a woman who was sick of feeling shortchanged and half alive.

I prayed and waited. And waited. Words spoken by the prophet Isaiah were my daily sustenance. A note posted on the bathroom mirror greeted me in the morning, reminding me that supernatural help was available: "But those who wait on the LORD will find new strength. They will fly on wings like eagles. They will run and not grow weary. They will walk and not faint" (Isaiah 40:31, NLT).

It didn't happen as fast as I would have liked. I learned that working through is *always* more of a struggle than walking out. But ever so slowly I began to feel drawn again to Aaron. Spontaneous surges of attraction and affection returned. I was surprised—pleasantly so.

That was ten years ago and what seems almost like another lifetime away. When I look at pictures from those years, I barely recognize the person staring back at me. So much has changed. Today my head and heart are in sync. My personal and professional lives are consistent and pure. And I have never been more in love with my husband.

—————

By God's grace, and a string of tough choices that redirected their energy toward one another, Aaron and Tamara have fully recovered from their dreadful wounds.

There are some elements in Tamara's story that all of us would be wise to glean. First, the physical anguish and spiritual estrangement she experienced as a result of her choices are not unusual. When we violate our own principles, the results on the body and spirit are nothing short of horrific.

Second, forgiveness—and recovery—is possible. God doesn't drop us because we drop Him. He is always waiting in the wings for our return. Remember the parable of the prodigal son? The heavenly Father has prodigal daughters, too.

Third, God is able and eager to help those who choose His ways. He will empower our prudent choices. He will galvanize good consequences because He is glad to bless wisdom at work.

Awhile back I read the splendid little book *Gift from the Sea* by Anne Morrow Lindbergh, wife of the international hero and American aviator, Charles Lindbergh. Anne is a remarkable woman whose exploits have equaled her husband's. Her brilliant mind is reflected in her poetry and essays, and in this particular book, Anne states her personal credo. Her views ring with a sense of authenticity and congruence:

> I want, first of all…to be at peace with myself. I want a singleness of eye, a purity of intention, a central core to my life that will enable me to carry out these obligations and activities as well as I can.
>
> I want in fact—to borrow from the language of the

saints—to live "in grace" as much of the time as possible. I am not using this term in a strictly theological sense. By grace I mean an inner harmony, essentially spiritual, which can be translated into outward harmony. I am seeking perhaps what Socrates asked for in the prayer from the Phaedrus when he said, "May the outward and the inward man be one." I would like to achieve a state of inner spiritual grace from which I could function and give as I was meant to in the eye of God.[1]

The bottom line? Anything shy of congruence between what we believe and how we live breeds chaos. And friend, worn-out women are sitting targets. Fatigue robs us of the ability to think straight. No matter how strong our relationship with God, we are *never* immune to temptation. Given the right circumstances, and the right time, anyone is vulnerable.

Tamara's story tells us:

- We have the freedom and ability to control our choices, but not the consequences.
- No matter how bad a mistake may be, we need to keep an open line to God. He's the One who can best help us untangle our mess.
- Feelings follow actions. We must do what we know is right, and trust that our heart will eventually catch up with our head.

- When problems arise in our relationships, we need to avoid the blame game and take responsibility for our own contributing behavior.
- When we violate our convictions, we sabotage our spirit.
- In truth, we can't have it all, and we can't do it all—at once. There is an appointed time for everything. Having quality of life is about choices.

I witnessed an intimate moment between Aaron and Tamara a while back. John and I were teaching, and they were attending, a marriage enrichment weekend getaway at a lovely hotel on the ocean. During one of the gatherings, Aaron presented Tamara with a beautiful hand-carved bald eagle, enclosed in glass. It was a symbol of his unconditional love and support and of her renewed loyalty to their partnership in life.

The message was clear: "Soar, Tamara, soar!" I'm delighted to tell you that's exactly what she's doing. And the love of her life is beside her all the way.

Power Perks: A SIP OF HOPE AND HUMOR

Church bulletin bloopers:

- "Miss Charlene Mason sang, 'I Will Not Pass This Way Again,' giving obvious pleasure to the congregation."
- "Ladies, don't forget the rummage sale. It is a good chance to get rid of those things not worth keeping around the house. Bring your husbands."
- "Smile at someone who is hard to love. Say 'hell' to someone who doesn't care much about you."
- "The sermon this morning: 'Jesus Walks on the Water.' The sermon tonight: 'Searching for Jesus.'"
- "Barbara C. remains in the hospital and needs blood donors for more transfusions. She is also having trouble sleeping and requests tapes of Pastor Jack's sermons."

God gave us free choice because there is no significance to love that knows no alternative.

James Dobson[2]

It is this way. The Lord, he is always voting for a man; and the devil, he is always voting against him. Then the man himself votes and breaks the tie.[3]

We have the freedom to take which course we choose, but not freedom to determine the end of that choice.

Oswald Chambers[4]

CHAPTER 16

Consult the Expert

I do nothing without consulting the Father.

John 5:30, NLT

It was one of those periods of restless indecision. We were confused, not knowing which direction was God's. The church we were serving in at the time was suffering a very difficult transition because the senior pastor was in the process of leaving. Although John had been on the church staff eight years and was fulfilled in his assignment, we were wondering if this would be a natural time for us to make a change too. Often when a new senior pastor is hired, many from the former regime are let go. We weren't sure what God had in mind for our future.

I was pregnant. With a baby on the way, John and I had talked about moving closer to our parents so that we could spend more time with them and give our children the privilege of growing up with their grandparents nearby. It just so happened that at the same time all the upheaval was happening at our church, a church not far from both of our families was scouting for an assistant pastor. A leader from that church contacted us, and we met with him to discuss the option.

At the close of that meeting the answer seemed obvious. On paper it was cut and dried: The pros of leaving our current church far outweighed the cons. The new position offered twice the salary for John, an open door for me to practice as a licensed therapist on the church staff, and close proximity to both sets of parents. The timing also seemed perfect. Any casual observer would have thought we were nuts for not jumping at the opportunity.

But something didn't seem right to us.

Neither John nor I had peace about saying yes to the move. I can't even give you a logical reason why—we just didn't feel the Lord's release to leave. We sought the Lord for direction and asked for wisdom. We told the Lord we would go wherever He wanted us to, but we needed Him to help us clearly hear His voice.

A certain verse held special meaning for us during that time: "I am the LORD your God, who teaches you what is good and leads you along the paths you should follow" (Isaiah 48:17, NLT).

About halfway through my pregnancy with Jessie, I developed a bad case of snoring that rudely invaded John's sleep. Consequently, sometime between midnight and dawn John usually groped his way through the dark into the spare bedroom so he could get his fair share of shut-eye. The poor guy was having his beauty sleep ripped off before this baby was even out of the womb.

One morning, just as the sun was beginning to peek through the gray Oregon clouds, John came in from the guest room and crawled back into bed with me. "I think I heard from the Lord," he whispered.

"Really?" I replied, trying to focus my sleepy eyes on him. "What did He say?"

"He said we're supposed to stay where we are."

In an instant I knew John was right. My spirit bore witness with his, and we both sensed a calm assurance that the direction was from the Lord.

I know—from a human standpoint it didn't make much sense. The out-of-town offer seemed to offer far more benefits. A series of unfortunate events, plus the departure of a much-loved pastor, had left our congregation wounded and grieving. Attending services was a drain because everywhere we turned, we heard grumbling and complaining. Some people leaned on us for comfort while others simply wanted to vent. Our church had turned from a consolation to a cauldron boiling with gossip and idle chatter. Tempers were hot. Fuses were short. People were burned. It was a painful season to weather. Leaving seemed a welcome escape to the path of blessing. But God was asking us to stay and endure hardship, trusting He knew what was best.

Soon after the Lord had given us direction, word came that a new pastor and his wife were coming to our church. We didn't know Ted and Diane Roberts, but we knew the Lord had asked us to stay and serve with them, so we did. That was fifteen years ago.

Hindsight offers clarity. Today we see clearly why God asked us to stay. It was His intention to restore the church and us, and He wanted us to have the joy of being a part of the healing process. Don't get me wrong; the path of healing wasn't easy. Wounded people need extra time, attention, and gentle care. Under the circumstances, John and I felt like physicians in an emergency room where the revolving door never stopped ushering in the injured. Being bombarded by so many needs—including our own—was taxing and called for every ounce of patience and perseverance that was in our reserves.

During the next several years, we had the privilege of watching God mend broken hearts. Fractures have been repaired. The church has grown from eight hundred to 6,500 people. Today those who were wounded are reaching out to others who have been assaulted by this world's hardships. Lives, including ours, have been profoundly influenced and forever changed by the healing power of God.

Yet I don't think I have ever been more grateful for God's leading in our lives than when I was speaking at a woman's conference a few years after the Lord had told us to "stay put." The retreat was held in the town adjacent to the city where we had considered relocating. During a break following a general session, I was standing in a circle, casually talking with a group of women. Clusters of ladies with Styrofoam cups of hot coffee in hand were visiting throughout the foyer. The groups stood fairly close together, so it wasn't difficult to hear what was being said around me.

There I was minding my own business, when all of a sudden I heard a woman behind me say, "Isn't it a tragedy what has happened at such-and-such church?" It was the church we had been invited to join! That's when I started eavesdropping on purpose. What I gleaned from the conversation just about stopped my heart. Apparently the church was falling apart because of some serious mistakes made by a couple of prominent people in leadership. The news deeply grieved me.

The coffee break ended, and I had to call upon every ounce of caffeine in my body to stay focused on my next seminar. I don't think the ladies in the foyer knew their conversation had reached my ears, but I believe the Lord allowed it. When I returned to my hotel room at the end of the day, I knelt beside my bed in humble reverence and said, "Thank You! Thank You! Thank You, Lord!"

It's sobering to think about what may have happened had we not sought the Lord in our decision-making process. It would have been so easy to do what *naturally* made sense. After all, we could have escaped a lot of heat had we left at that time.

But it would have been a huge mistake with far-reaching consequences. We would have been relying on our own finite efforts to get us out of that mess. We would have been trusting in our limited human reasoning and abilities instead of on the Spirit's guidance and timing. In the process we would have cut ourselves off from an extensive and beautiful work of God's grace in our lives.

We see now how consulting the Father spared us misery upon misery. Had we relocated, we would have gone from one broken church congregation into another. I'm not certain we would have survived those stresses very well. I'm so grateful for God's mercy.

It makes sense to weigh the pros and cons when making a decision. But one thing I have learned through the years is that we must never stop there. Even if an answer seems obvious to the human mind, it may not be the divine course of action. We can save ourselves much weariness and grief if we stop and consult the Expert. Though the direction He gives may involve rough waters, His counsel is *always* in our best interest.

For only God sees the big picture.

Only God knows the future, and the full implications of our decisions.

Only God can detect when an apparent escape hatch is a death trap in disguise.

Only God knows what will fulfill and restore the darkest depths of our soul.

Only God knows when, where, and how the flames in this world will run their course.

In His mercy, He is eager to lead us on. We can be confident that the guidance He gives will always be for our highest good.

Even if it means enduring the heat a little while longer.

Power Perks: A Sip of Hope and Humor

One day a group of scientists got together and decided that man had come a long way and no longer needed God. So they picked one scientist to go and tell Him that they were done with Him.

The scientist walked up to God and said, "God, we've decided that we no longer need You. We're to the point that we can clone people and do many miraculous things, so why don't You just go on and get lost?"

God listened very patiently and kindly to the man. After the scientist was done talking, God said, "Very well. How about this? Let's say we have a man-making contest."

The scientist replied, "Okay, great!"

But God added, "Now, we're going to do this just like I did back in the old days with Adam."

The scientist said, "Sure, no problem" and bent down and grabbed himself a handful of dirt.

God looked at him and said, "No, no, no. You go get your own dirt!"

God's heavenly plan doesn't always make earthly sense.

Charles Swindoll[1]

There are two kinds of people: those who say to God, "Thy will be done," and those to whom God says, "All right, then, have it your way."

C. S. Lewis[2]

Where God has put a period, do not change it to a question mark.

T. J. Bach[3]

CHAPTER 17

Forgiveness Is Supernatural

or if you forgive people their trespasses—that is, their reckless and willful sins, leaving them, letting them go and giving up resentment—your heavenly Father will also forgive you.

Matthew 6:14, AMP

I'm convinced that nothing will kill a woman's spirit faster than holding on to resentment. And nothing will dissolve bitterness more effectively than choosing to forgive.

If you have borne the arrows of betrayal, the shrapnel of lies, the hand grenade of public humiliation, you know the disintegration that can result from one person's selfish choices. But do you know the healing bandages of Jesus, who was called the Balm of Gilead? Do you know the tender hands of the skillful Surgeon who can remove any dis-ease? Have you experienced the sweet release of forgiveness made possible by the Spirit's soothing?

Meet Nancy, who has endured one of the harshest spiritual wars known to humankind and emerged whole—because the Medic intervened.

It all started when their eyes met.

He's looking at me! she thought excitedly.

Her stomach turned flip-flops, and her heart thumped so hard she thought it would burst. But she didn't let on. Nonchalantly, she turned back to the book she had been reading and secretly wondered, *Could the big man on campus actually be interested in me?*

Nancy was a typical collegiate: young, pretty, full of dreams, idealistic, somewhat naïve. She had a number of good friends, was academically strong, and held leadership positions. Even so, she thought Doug was way out of her league. He was the kind of guy who had it all. Handsome, athletic, and funny, he was also graced with a charisma that drew a crowd like a magnet. That's why she was shocked later that evening when she heard his voice on the other end of the line asking her to go to dinner.

That first date led to countless others, and soon Nancy and Doug were in love. Nancy was thrilled but a little scared. She knew that if she ever lost Doug's interest, a dozen eager females would gladly take her place. So she resolved to do whatever it took to keep him.

Doug was passionate in his pursuit of intimacy very early in their relationship, and Nancy complied. There were times when they resolved to slow down, but surging hormones won. They made promises they didn't keep, and Nancy began feeling more like an object being used than a woman being loved. But she worshiped the ground Doug walked on and couldn't imagine life without him. Her guilt seemed like a small price to pay.

The young couple finally set a wedding date. Nancy still carried a gnawing sense that something wasn't right but shrugged it off as prewedding jitters. She figured every bride had similar reservations that eventually faded away.

But hers didn't.

To everyone's shock—even her own—she called off the wedding a week before she and Doug were to marry.

The couple had originally planned to move after the wedding to New Jersey, where Doug was registered at Princeton Seminary. As it turned out, he left for the East Coast alone, and Nancy stayed behind in California. Her head told her something was missing in their relationship, but her heart was sick with fear over the possibility of losing him. They talked every day on the phone. Nancy even visited him once. Then she received the horrific news from her doctor: She was pregnant.

Nancy's parents were devastated, and she figured the best

way to erase their disappointment was to walk down the aisle and make things "legal." Though initially reluctant, Doug eventually agreed to do "the right thing." Being young, idealistic, and armed with a personal resolve to make the relationship work, Nancy dismissed her earlier doubts. The couple married, returned to New Jersey, and set up house. Doug studied and worked. Nancy hung wallpaper in the nursery and did the other things most young mothers do when the nesting instinct prevails.

On the outside, things appeared relatively normal. But inside, a nagging ache told Nancy that something was profoundly amiss. She couldn't define the problem in specific terms but did try to talk with Doug about it. He always had a ready answer and blamed her frustration on deadlines, term papers, his work, and the pregnancy, which, he said, made her overly sensitive. His explanations made sense. Nancy told herself to "get a grip" and try harder.

A daughter was born, and for several months Nancy was enraptured in being a new mother. Doug was a proud father, showing off his little girl to anyone who dropped over to the house. The couple oohed and ahhed, burped and bounced, and filled scrapbooks with joyful snapshots of their little pink bundle.

There were many who helped them celebrate—friends, neighbors, and fellow students. A woman who worked with Doug often stopped by. She had a one-year-old son, and Nancy eagerly asked her some young-mother questions. One evening after the woman left, Nancy felt strangely uncomfortable. She didn't know why—nothing unusual had occurred that night. When Nancy mentioned her feelings to Doug, he dismissed them as postpartum depression and said she should be grateful for a friend with whom she could swap parenting strategies. Nancy assumed it was just homesickness and chose to believe that after Doug graduated and they returned to California, things would be fine.

Once back on the West Coast, the couple did enjoy a fresh start. Doug started a new job. Nancy was determined to make life good. They finally had some extra money and a little free time. They settled into a new routine that revolved around his work, their family, friends, and church.

Doug's job required some evenings and weekends away. As these increased in frequency, Nancy shrugged off his absence to the demands of corporate America and focused on their daughter. It always helped when loved ones came to visit. Becky, a good friend from New Jersey, flew out for a week. She said she was having some marriage problems and needed a place to get away and think. Since Doug had taken many classes in counseling and was gifted in helping couples in trouble, he spent hours talking with her. Around one o'clock one morning, Nancy awoke and realized he wasn't in bed next to her. When she found Becky and Doug talking in the living room, he said he was trying to help her sort through some issues and that he would be along shortly. Nancy returned to bed, thinking, *What is wrong with me? How could I begrudge my friend the help she needs?*

The next day, when Doug took Becky to see his office, Nancy and the baby, who was fussy, stayed home. Her fearful suspicions returned. On one hand, something seemed amiss; on the other, her fears seemed irrational. Nancy went into her bedroom and began to cry, softly at first, and then in gasping sobs. The depth and intensity of the pain left her doubled over and completely confused.

When Doug and Becky returned a couple of hours later, Nancy felt certain her fears had substance—that something had happened between them. And after Becky caught her flight home, Nancy questioned Doug about his involvement with her. He exploded in a rage and called her crazy. Again, she somehow put aside her convictions and believed him.

Yet something inside Nancy died that day. She heard Doug's words, but she knew they were lies. She was tormented by a grotesque reality she didn't know how to process. She hated Doug and she loved Doug—what could she do?

Another daughter came along. Doug continued to work long hours, yet in many ways he was a good husband. He helped around the house and stayed with the girls once in a while so that Nancy could go out with friends. Now and then he even brought her flowers and little gifts. Nancy was the envy of the women who knew the couple.

As the years passed, other incidents caused Nancy to ques-

tion Doug's faithfulness. Every time she confronted him, he rec-
ommended that she get professional treatment for her raging
paranoia. Nancy felt as if her head and heart were at war. There
were times when she honestly wondered if she was losing her
mind. She begged Doug for the truth, no matter how painful,
but he continued to deny any wrongdoing.

Finally, one evening after Nancy had put the children to bed,
Doug called her to the living room. In a single mind-blowing
conversation, he confirmed Nancy's worst fears. He had, in fact,
made love with Becky when she was visiting in their home. Then
he confessed to one affair after another. Nancy learned of a relationship Doug had had with another woman during their
engagement and which had continued for two years after their
marriage. He spoke of a coworker he had had a liaison with for
several years. It was the woman from his office who had the one-
year-old child. She had been Nancy's dear friend.

Nancy's response? I'll let her tell you the rest in her own
words.

My soul froze over in icy anger. I had spent several long years
questioning myself and doubting my perceptions. I had wasted
precious energy shaming myself for being suspicious. Doug's
confessions blew my world apart like sticks of dynamite.
Resentment and bitterness smothered me beneath their load. I

seriously wondered if I would ever be able to dig my way out from under these realities.

I'm not sure what prompted Doug to tell me everything, except that he thought it was "the right thing" to do. From that vantage point I think he confessed strictly to assuage his guilt. Shortly thereafter he decided to move out. Since we couldn't afford two residences on his income, I was forced to look for a job, which was not an easy assignment. My marketable skills were poor because for the last eight years I had devoted myself to staying home with the children.

I remember reading the Bible and wondering where God was in this mess. I read stories of God's healing and grace and thought, *What a crock! These words must have been written by people who were out of touch with reality.* It was hard for me to trust anyone, much less God. I did a fine job of protecting myself from Him and everyone else with a shield of angry detachment. The only one I allowed anywhere near my heart was my best friend, Karen.

Karen stayed close in this dark valley. She prayed for me each day. She talked of God's love and of her high hopes for my future. She listened to me. She cried with me. She did not judge me. And she didn't tell me what to do.

During our separation, Doug visited the children periodically for a few hours at a time. They were broken by the sorrow of our fragmented marriage and the uncertainty of the ongoing separation. In the midst of that miserable period, I took inventory. It included a long, hard look at me. I remember crying in a heap on the bathroom floor, asking God to change me. I begged Him for strength to cope with the bone-crushing weariness that came from my unrelenting efforts to hold our family together.

I also asked God to heal the pervasive suspicion and fear that had consumed me. Healing began when I was completely honest and said *God, I don't trust You, but I see people who do and I WANT to.* I knew deep down that God was the only One who had the answers. I prayed for His power to heal our marriage and restore our family. I figured if He could resurrect the dead, He could birth new life in my broken relationship with Doug. I asked for wisdom to know what to do. More than anything I wanted what was best for the children.

It wasn't long after I had said those prayers that Doug started bringing a female friend with him to visit the children. That same week I found a letter a distant cousin had written to Doug. The content was personal and vaguely sexual. I confronted Doug and my cousin, and as usual, things were explained away. I had been in this place before, and my heart told me I wasn't hearing the truth. When I hung up the phone, I knew God's hands were tied. He could not heal where dishonesty reigned. Lies were blocking His miracles.

Eventually the blinders were lifted from my eyes, and I could see that I was absolutely powerless over Doug's choices. I filed for divorce and chose to remain silent about Doug's infidelity. People questioned why I couldn't forgive him for making "one" mistake. Surely, they thought, we could have worked things out. Trying my best to go on without Doug, I slammed the door on the guilt over filing for divorce and the unresolved grief over losing our family. But stuffing the pain didn't make it go away. It just made matters worse.

I had long, angry talks with God. I asked Him where He was when my husband was betraying me and why He hadn't protected the children and me from this abuse. I told Him how desperately unsafe I felt in this God-forsaken world. I wondered about the next shoe He planned to drop.

All the while, God listened patiently and continued sending blessings that were difficult for me to see through the fog of my grief.

I was so overcome with the injustice the children and I had suffered that vengeance seemed like a practical and logical solution. If I just opened my mouth and told all, I could have destroyed Doug.

But something constrained me.

Actually, Someone constrained me.

The Spirit of God began to speak to me about letting go of my bitterness. Suddenly, everywhere I turned, somebody was saying something about forgiveness: The lady on *The Oprah Winfrey Show*. The song on the radio. The preacher at church. My friend on the phone. They were all delivering the same message:

"Forgive."

Forgive? I cried to God. *Impossible! How do I forgive someone who doesn't deserve forgiveness?*

"You pray."

But God, I don't want to pray for Doug. I don't want to pray for his sideline attractions. They betrayed me. I will hate them forever!

"Not if you pray for them."

It was about then that Karen gave me a book on the difficulties of suffering injustice. As I read, I came face-to-face with a set of choices. I could either continue my descent into bitterness and resentment, or I could admit my inability to God. I wrestled with these ideas for months before I was able to admit to God that I couldn't continue on my own. I needed God to give me supernatural strength to do what He had asked me to do—to pray for those who had betrayed me.

Moments of fleeting relief came as I journaled my uncensored feelings in a daily diary. Revealing the most intimate details of my life helped purge the pain. In my quiet times, I read about a man named Job who was able to put words to the anguish I was feeling. I found solace in his life story and in the fact that God was the One who had the final word in his life. Not his friends. Not his family. Not his acquaintances. It gave me hope to know that God's last word in Job's life was one of total restoration.

The injustices I suffered from my husband's sexual addiction stole my sense of worth and personal dignity. But looking back,

I can see that the bitterness I hung on to for several years robbed me of the ability to heal and move forward. A turning point came when I realized that I could not afford to leave unchecked the hatred simmering in my heart.

I had to acknowledge that what happened to me *happened.* I was not crazy. I had to face the facts and grieve the reality of the injustice if I was ever going to be able to move beyond it. Somewhere along the line I heard someone say that if we all lived by the rule "an eye for an eye," the whole world would be blind. It reminded me of the many mistakes I had made in my life and of God's unending compassion and grace in forgiving me. How could I not forgive when God had forgiven me of so much?

I made a conscious choice to let go of my quest for justice for Doug and the women who had betrayed me. I felt nothing. But I did what I knew God had told me to do months before. I prayed for them and released them into God's hands. From that day forward I decided it wasn't my job to set them straight or make them pay. Their wrongs were between them and God. My energies were focused on my own health and the well-being of my children.

Months later I received confirmation, through an odd twist of events, that Doug had, in fact, been intimate with my second cousin. But the information didn't pack much punch. It was old news. I knew it had happened years ago, and I had already chosen to forgive them.

I was amazed by the insignificant impact this information

had on me. Forgiveness had already begun diluting the poison in my heart. I felt no hatred. No bitterness. No desire for revenge. I felt only sadness for a man who appeared to have it all together on the outside, but who so obviously had lost his way.

To this day, I have moments when the past sweeps in like a raging river and leaves me gasping for air. Forgiveness didn't come easily or quickly. But it came. I learned that if we merely call a spade a spade, forgiveness is often unattainable from a human standpoint. But when you factor in the divine, all things are possible. God supernaturally empowered me to release my death grip on rage and let it go.

Once I told the Lord that I was willing to forgive, my spirit reopened to His Spirit. I began to sense that God was touched by my pain, that He had taken up my cause, and that He held both Doug and me in His hands. He would have the final say in both of our lives. Eventually I stopped striving for justice and embraced the peace that only God could give.

While forgiving Doug didn't have much impact on him, it has made all the difference in the world for the girls and me. Forgiveness was a gift we gave ourselves. We have moved on with our lives, and we are no longer controlled by our losses. There is life beyond betrayal. And it's a *good* life, filled with an abundance of God's richest blessings. Job's story is true—I'm living it!

If we want to snip the soul ties that keep us in bondage…

If we want to take back the dignity that has been stolen from us…

If we want God to heal the holes in our soul…

If we want to douse the flames of bitter revenge…

If we want something good to come out of something very, very bad…we must choose to forgive. It's God's way. And when He has His way, war-torn people become whole. Peace reigns. And pain evaporates into praise.

Do you need a divine Medic today?

Power Perks: A Sip of Hope and Humor

Dumbwaiter: One who asks if the kids would care to order dessert.

Family Planning: The art of spacing the births of your children so you won't experience financial disaster.

Feedback: The inevitable result when the baby doesn't appreciate the strained carrots.

Full Name: What you call your child by when you're mad at him.

Grandparents: The people who think your children are wonderful even though they're sure you're not raising them right.

Impregnable: A woman whose memory of labor is still vivid.

Independent: How we want our children to be as long as they do everything we say.

Ow: The first word spoken by children with older siblings.

Prenatal: When your life was still somewhat your own.

Puddle: A small body of water that draws other small bodies wearing dry shoes into it.

Show-off: A child who is more talented than yours is.

Sterilize: What you do to your first baby's pacifier by boiling it and to your last baby's pacifier by blowing on it.

Top Bunk: Where you should never put a child wearing Superman jammies.

Whodunit: None of the kids who live in your house.

Forgiveness is not an occasional act, it is a permanent attitude.

Martin Luther King Jr.[1]

As we practice the work of forgiveness we discover more and more that forgiveness and healing are one.

Agnes Sanford[2]

Dress in the wardrobe God picked out for you: compassion, kindness, humility, quiet strength, discipline.... Forgive as quickly and completely as the Master forgave you. And regardless of what else you put on, wear love. It's your basic, all-purpose garment. Never be without it.

Colossians 3:12–14, MSG

CHAPTER 18

Christmas Chaos

*D*on't long for "the good old days,"
for you don't know whether they were any better than these!

Ecclesiastes 7:10, TLB

Even as an adult, Jill loved Christmas. Around December first she became a kid again, so enthralled in the wonder and excitement of the season that she could hardly contain herself. Traditions enhanced every aspect of the holidays, the biggest one being the family's Christmas Eve pilgrimage to her folks' house on the other side of town. This was the biggest event of the year. It didn't matter whether your own house was decorated or not, or that you still had umpteen things left to do. Grandma and Grandpa's house was where the action was, and no one in her right mind wanted to be left out of the fun. Their house was also where Santa left his loot. So if you didn't show up, you missed out big-time.

Then there was the lip-smacking, mouthwatering food. Grandma always served a delectable ham complemented by her famous potato salad and, of course, her home-canned, dilled green beans. They were such a delicacy that friends and relatives from near and far requested them for gifts. And dessert? You'd never seen so many scrumptious, fresh-baked, and elaborately decorated cookies under one roof. Grandma and the ladies in the clan had a cookie bake each year and artistically shaped each delicious treat.

There was a magical quality about Grandma and Grandpa's house during the holidays. It was more than the festively adorned house; more than the way the tree lights sparkled like diamonds against the deep forest greens. It was more than the way the carefully hung ornaments evoked memories of days gone by. The magic came from the enormous sense of love that hit full force when you walked in the front door. It was so real you could almost touch it. Worries evaporated, and everything seemed right with the world when you were at Grandma and Grandpa's on Christmas Eve.

Enter Christmas, 1983. It had been a tough year for Jill, her husband, Theo, and the kids. The couple had weathered some major changes personally and professionally. In a nutshell, Jill was worn out, and she had trouble getting into the Christmas spirit. She put off decorating and shopping until the very last minute and then did a halfhearted job. But she thought, *If I can just get to Mom and Dad's on Christmas Eve, everything will be better.*

Christmas Eve dawned, and beautiful, nickel-sized white flakes softly fell from the sky. "Wonderful!" Jill exclaimed happily, "we're going to have a white Christmas!" But by three o'clock the gentle flurries had turned into a ghastly blizzard. The roads were treacherous, and news commentators admonished people to stay off the streets unless they had a dire emergency. Televised footage of the city showed pictures of traffic ground to a halt.

But Jill, Theo, and the kids weren't going to miss Grandma and Grandpa's party for anything. Jill called her dad to check the road conditions on their side of town. "They're slick, honey, but I think you can make it if you're careful," he advised.

With determination they set out. The family loaded the trunk to the lid with gifts, and the boys squeezed into the back seat. Theo drove them first to the oldest son's workplace to pick him up. But by the time they reached him, it was obvious that it would be impossible to drive to the other side of town. The road was a sheet of ice and visibility was nil as wind whipped wet snow against the windshield. Theo broke the news: "We're not driving in this mess. We'll just have to spend Christmas Eve at home."

He turned the car around, and they crept back home at three miles per hour (on the straight shots), with Jill complaining every inch of the way. "Some Christmas this will be," she grumbled. "We don't even have any food in the house! I didn't bake a single batch of cookies!"

"Boys, be on the lookout for a restaurant where we can get a bite to eat," Theo replied.

Most everything was closed because of the holidays and the bad snowstorm. Finally Ted shouted from the back seat, "Dad, there's a place that's open!"

Jill took one look at the pizza restaurant and rolled her eyes. "Pizza? *For Christmas?* You've got to be kidding!"

By this time, Theo's patience was running thin, and he said quietly, "Pizza is better than nothing. We're stopping."

Reluctantly the troops forged through the snow and stomped their shoes clean inside the restaurant. Somewhere between the car and the counter, Jill's thoughts took a turn...for the better. *Come on now,* she encouraged herself. *Things aren't all bad. Just make the best of it.*

With two warm pizzas in hand, the family braved the elements once again. The roads were frighteningly slick, and they were thankful to get home without any mishaps. When the garage door finally closed behind them, they all uttered a huge sigh of relief.

The phone was ringing when they walked in the back door. It was Grandpa saying, "Don't even try to come! The roads are too dangerous!"

Theo built a fire in the fireplace, and the living room took on a warm, cozy glow. The family enjoyed a pizza picnic. Christmas music filled the air while they opened gifts. As they read the account of Jesus' wondrous birth, Jill sensed the Spirit impressing her to relish the moments they were sharing together. She suddenly realized that her sons wouldn't be living at home much longer, and that this evening was a gift. In fact, in a few years she might be the grandma whose house everyone would be visiting for Christmas Eve.

Following the infamous "Pizza Christmas" of 1983, things did change. Before Jill and Theo could blink, all three of their sons had brought home beautiful "daughters." The family continued its annual trek to the other side of town to celebrate Christmas Eve at Grandma and Grandpa's until the arrival of Olivia and Emma, the first two grandchildren. Thereafter, the Johnson gathering was held at Jill and Theo's. Grandma and Grandpa joined Jill and Theo on Christmas Day.

Jill assumed the role of Grandma with royal style. She, like her mom, decorated from stem to stern and shopped till she dropped. The formal dining room table was set with her finest china and silver. It looked *Victoria*-magazine elegant, right down to the unobtrusive high chair and booster seat for the little ones. Dinner included prime rib with all the trimmings, Great-Grandma's pickled beans, desserts galore, popcorn balls for the kids, and more. The dining room was a bit crowded, but it looked great. It seemed worth the effort to stay up half the night washing the china so that Grandma and Grandpa could eat in style with them the next day.

As the years passed, two more granddaughters and twin grandsons joined the clan. Christmas Eve became more complicated. Mommies were nursing or heating bottles for their babies. The toddlers were darting to and fro, picking up anything they could get their hands on, including Jill's porcelain collectibles. Jill and the young mothers spent much of their time policing decorations that were irresistible but hazardous to little fingers and mouths.

There were diapers to change, bibs to tie, and crying babies that needed to be held. The dining room was absolutely stuffed with multiple high chairs, booster seats, and a kiddie-style table with chairs. Once everyone sat down, no one could move. Still, they never were able to orchestrate everyone eating at the same time.

In 1997, after the Christmas Eve festivities were over and the house was quiet, Jill and Theo realized that they never did get around to reading the Christmas story. Opening presents took too long, and the little ones in attendance, high on holiday goodies, had taken the celebration to a new level. There may have been "peace on earth" somewhere in the world, but it definitely wasn't at their house!

The following morning, Jill sat in a sea of crumpled gift wrap and smashed ribbons, wondering, *What happened?* She was relieved her parents were spending that day with her brother's family. Theo reassured her that she wasn't losing her mind. She was just worn out. She had tried to do too much, with too little help from the rest of the family. It wasn't that they hadn't offered—Jill just wanted to spare them any extra burdens and figured she could do it all.

After the new year was well underway, and after much thought, Jill came to a fresh (if startling) conclusion: *Traditions don't have to be carved in granite.* She determined that some flexibility might buy her some sanity. So she talked with her children about what they liked and didn't like about the holidays. With God's help she was able to set aside her unrealistic expectations and even some of her family traditions. As they exchanged ideas, they came up with a new game plan.

Christmas Eve would be different. They decided to have a potluck buffet and to serve the food on paper plates. (The fine china would be reserved for Christmas Day when Grandma and Grandpa came to visit.) The daughters-in-law would bring some of their favorite recipes to add to Jill's lineup of goodies. People would eat what they wanted, where they wanted, and when they wanted. Presents would be opened at the beginning of the evening so the children would have plenty of toys to keep them busy. Meanwhile, the adults could spend the evening relaxing by the fire, singing carols, and playing games. Theo would pull out his well-worn Bible and, in keeping with tradition, read Luke's account of the Nativity.

Long story short: That year Christmas Eve at the Johnson

household was a smashing success. Even though the agenda had been modified, the most important elements of their family traditions were maintained: They were all together as a family; the Christmas story was a focal point; the food was delicious; and Santa delivered his loot. It was a lively, fun-filled evening, and all seemed right with the world at Grandpa Theo and Grandma Jill's. Flexibility paid.

What about your house? Are your holidays festive and fun, or occasions for dramatic overdoing? Try Jill's recipe for worn-out women suffering Christmas chaos. With the help of your family, take a fresh look at the traditions you feel you must keep. See if you can modify a few and consider if more hands wouldn't make less work.

Let flexibility make peace possible.

Goodwill always follows.

Power Perks: A Sip of Hope and Humor

Question: Do you know what would have happened if it had been three Wise Women instead of three Wise Men?

Answer: They would have asked directions, arrived on time, helped deliver the baby, cleaned the stable, made a casserole, and brought practical gifts.

Better to bend than break.[1]

It is Christmas every time you let God love others through you...yes, it is Christmas every time you smile at your brother and offer him your hand.

Mother Teresa of Calcutta[2]

Once a year and only once, the whole world stands still to celebrate the advent of a life. Only Jesus claims this worldwide, undying remembrance.[3]

Christmas is not a date. It is a state of mind.

Mary Ellen Chase[4]

Keep changing. When you're through changing, you're through.

Bruce Barton[5]

CHAPTER 19

God's Math

I tell you the truth, whatever you did for one of the least of these brothers of mine, you did for me.

Matthew 25:40

For years Julie and Tim have served as foster parents to drug-addicted and high-risk infants. Baby Sandra was one of many who have left an indelible mark on their lives.

Sandra suffered many problems from severe alcohol exposure during pregnancy. The doctor who delivered the baby said the mother's amniotic fluid actually smelled like alcohol. Sandra cried around the clock for the first few months—talk about a setup for the Worn-out-Woman Syndrome! But Julie and her family lovingly nursed the little one to health. And six months later, a wonderful, stable family decided to adopt Sandra.

The day arrived for baby Sandra to go home with her new mother and father. Just as the adoptive couple was leaving,

Sandra's father-to-be stopped, turned the wheelchair he was sitting in around and handed Julie a cassette. It was a tape of some of his favorite songs. He knew it was difficult for Julie and her family to say good-bye to Sandra, and he wanted, in some small way, to encourage them. This man obviously had many challenges of his own, and music, he said, brought joy to his soul.

As the couple drove off with Sandra strapped safely in her infant carrier, Julie walked back into the house to find her daughters, Katie and Karissa, wiping away tears. They had loved Sandra day and night for six months, and it was hard to see her go. Julie reminded them of the awesome privilege they had of helping an abandoned drug-addicted, pain-filled infant become a chubby, healthy, happy baby embraced by a mommy and daddy who were thrilled to give her a loving home.

The following day Julie received an unexpected call from the local children's shelter, asking if she could pick up a nameless newborn who had been left on the shelter doorstep. Julie wasn't sure how to respond. The night before she and Tim had decided to take a break after sending Sandra on her way. But the couple's need for a time-out seemed tiny compared to the baby boy's need for a nurturing home, so she agreed. She decided to tell Tim later.

Around six o'clock that evening, Tim came home to find Julie giving a tiny newborn with thick black hair a much-needed bath in their sink. He could see at a glance that the baby hadn't been close to soap and water for days. Propping himself against the counter, Tim listened to the story behind the surprise visitor. They guessed the little guy was about two months old. Like Julie, Tim quickly found a warm spot in his heart for this nameless, homeless little boy. In fact the baby's circumstances reminded him of another infant who had appeared suddenly without friend or family. "Since the shelter staff found him on their doorstep, how about calling him Moses?" Tim suggested.

The girls agreed. Katie snapped a picture, and the entire family took turns holding baby Moses through the evening.

The next morning Julie checked on Moses during his nap and found him sleeping peacefully. Saturdays were usually work-around-the-house day, so everyone was busy with projects. The girls completed their chores, then asked to go shopping. Julie had some errands to run, too, so she gathered a few items for the diaper bag and went to get Moses. But when she picked him up, his mouth fell open, and he didn't startle like babies usually do. She tickled him, thinking she could rouse him out of his deep sleep, but there was no response. With her heart beating wildly, Julie raced to the kitchen where the kids were watching TV and yelled, "Get Daddy! The baby is dead." She quickly dialed 911.

Tim ran into the house, washed his hands, and started CPR. Moses' color was good. He just looked as if he were in a deep sleep. Tim worked frantically. Suddenly the baby began coughing up bloody mucus. As Tim wiped the baby's mouth with his fingers, the thought crossed Julie's mind that Moses might be HIV positive. The shelter had had no clue where this baby had come from, much less his medical history.

Paramedics arrived and started working on baby Moses. Rapid-fire questions ensued.

"How old is this baby?"

"We don't know."

"What is his name?"

"We don't know. We call him Moses. He just arrived from the shelter last night. He's a foster baby."

Then police rang the doorbell. The officers wanted to see the baby's bed. More accusatory questions followed. Finally one of the officers called in his report, and Julie heard him say, "It doesn't look like there is anything suspicious here."

Suspicious? she thought. *What does he mean by that? Our home is safe! It's a place of protective custody. It is not where babies die!*

The scene was almost too much for Julie to grasp. The paramedics were working feverishly to revive Moses in the family room. Katie and Karissa were crying. One of the police officers was wiping tears off his face, too. He had never been called in on a SIDS case before.

The paramedics tried everything: still no brainwaves, still no heartbeat. Julie followed the ambulance to the hospital while Tim stayed at home with the girls. When she arrived at the medical center, a staff person guided her to a private waiting room. A few minutes later a doctor offered condolences. Baby

Moses was gone, a victim of crib death.

Though Julie had known the little boy less than twenty-four hours, she broke down and cried as if he had been her own. The staff allowed Julie to spend some time with baby Moses. She ran her fingers through his long black hair one final time. She noticed that his color had dramatically changed during the time it took to reach the hospital. She realized she had likely picked him up from his crib within seconds of his passing.

As Julie drove home, questions darted through her mind. *Why did this have to happen? What about Tim? Has he been exposed to HIV? Should we have left baby Moses at the shelter? Were we wrong to bring him home with us? Should we be caring for infants at all?*

Once home, Julie delivered the sad news to her family. Without an ounce of energy left for anyone, she drew a warm bath, and grabbed her tape player and the first handy cassette. It was the tape Sandra's father had left the day before. Sinking into the comforting warmth of the bath water, Julie heard the words from an old hymn, "There will be peace in the valley...." She prayed it would be true.

The following day Julie and Tim talked with numerous doctors about the possibility of HIV exposure. They all agreed that Tim should see an infectious disease doctor, who counseled him to get a hepatitis gamma globulin shot. They waited for an autopsy report to determine whether baby Moses had carried HIV, but it seemed as if everyone's hands were tied up in red tape.

Who was this baby? Julie wondered.

Again, Julie questioned her and Tim's "calling" as foster parents. Fear gripped her soul. As days passed and no word came, Julie felt as if she was teetering on the edge of sanity. Besides grieving Moses' death, she felt enormous guilt for bringing this suffering on her family. *If only I had said no to the shelter…If only I had stuck to our original decision to take a break…If only I had let the shelter find another family.* Sheer desperation made her cry out to God for strength and assurance.

A few days later, Carol, the social services representative, stopped by. She wanted to give Tim and Julie updated information about the mysterious little boy who had visited their family. "The police have located the baby's parents," Carol reported. "We know that his name was Moses."

Tim and Julie looked at each other, astounded. Coincidence? Julie knew better. In an instant she knew that God was with their family and that she had not made a mistake in bringing this baby home. Finding out they had named the baby by his real name was the beam of light Julie had pleaded for in the dark. Suddenly a bigger picture came into view. Julie realized that God had orchestrated events so that little Moses spent his last night on earth showered with attention, surrounded by the warmth of loving faces and eager arms, encompassed in the love of a family who called him by name. Julie and Tim had had the privilege of being Moses' last stop on his way to heaven.

Incidentally, Moses means "to be drawn out," and so he was: first from the cold doorstep of homelessness, then from a frail physical body.

Julie was "drawn out" too—drawn out of her fears and guilt, her uncertainty and pain. Moses wasn't the first infant who had brought trauma to her family. Foster parenting exacted a price each time she obeyed. But for the first time she realized that the results of her foster parenting were not as important as her continued submission to the Father's call.

Weeks passed. Tim and Julie eventually heard from authorities that all the medical reports indicated Moses had not carried HIV. And yes, the next time the shelter called, Julie responded quickly, "Yes, we'll take him. When can we pick him up?"

I think it's safe to say that most of us wouldn't blame Tim and Julie for wanting to give up foster parenting after such a traumatic incident. A natural response would be retreat to avoid more heartache. But there is nothing remotely natural about this family's mission of mercy. It is Spirit driven and God empowered. Look at what the Bible says:

> I want you to share your food with the hungry and bring right into your own homes those who are helpless, poor and destitute. Clothe those who are cold and don't hide from relatives who need your help.

If you do these things, God will shed his own glorious light upon you. He will heal you; your godliness will lead you forward, and goodness will be a shield before you, and the glory of the Lord will protect you from behind. Then, when you call, the Lord will answer. "Yes, I am here," he will quickly reply.…

And the Lord will guide you continually, and satisfy you with all good things, and keep you healthy too; and you will be like a well-watered garden, like an ever-flowing spring. (Isaiah 58:7–9, 11, TLB)

That's why Moses' abrupt exit from this world didn't stop Tim and Julie. If we know we are doing what we are gifted and commanded to do, we can actually be replenished by pouring out. We can receive in the midst of giving. And we can see God's resources fill in where human ones fail. In God's mathematics, the more we give, the more we have to give—like ever-flowing mountain springs that don't run dry. This is why the Bowman home continues to be a place where rivers of healing flow. Since Moses' exit, dozens of other needy babies have been nursed to health in the gentle arms of Tim and Julie and their girls.

What's in your cup? Do you have some time, talents, or resources you can share with others? Why not risk, purposely pass your cup, and share some sips with those in need today? When the Lord is doing the filling, there's always more than enough to go around.

Power Perks: A Sip of Hope and Humor

A woman was gliding along the interstate in her new BMW on a relaxing evening drive. The top was down, the breeze was blowing through her hair, and she decided to open her up.

As the speedometer needle jumped up to eighty, then ninety, then one hundred miles per hour, she suddenly saw flashing red-and-blue lights behind her. She sighed and pulled over.

The officer approached, took her license, and examined it and the car. "Look," he said, weariness in his voice, "it's been a long day. This is the end of my shift, and it's Friday. I don't feel like creating more paperwork, so if you can give me an excuse for speeding that I haven't heard before, you can go."

The lady thought for a second. She looked at the officer, smiled, and said, "Last week my husband ran off with one of your lady officers. I was afraid you were trying to give him back."

The policeman handed back her license and turned toward his car, saying, "Have a nice day."

It is not my ability but my response to God's ability that counts.

Corrie ten Boom[1]

You can give without love, but you cannot love without giving.

Amy Carmichael[2]

"You're blessed when you're at the end of your rope. With less of you there is more of God and his rule."

Matthew 5:2, MSG

Acceptance of what has happened is the first step to overcoming the consequences of any misfortune.

William James[3]

CHAPTER 20
Living by God's Clock

*I am sure that God who began the good work within you
will keep right on helping you grow in his grace
until his task within you is finally finished.*

Philippians 1:6, TLB

Julee's eyes twinkle as a smile spreads across her face. "Pam, these are the joys that keep me going," she says. She's just finished rummaging through some things on her desk and is pointing to a stack of snapshots. They're wedding pictures, taken just a week ago, of her daughter, Merry, and new son-in-law, Nicholas.

Anyone looking at the pictures would never guess the wedding was planned in three weeks. From the elaborate decorations in the sanctuary, to the intricate details of the fine-tuned ceremony, to the gala atmosphere of the reception, you'd think the family had spent at least a year getting ready for the big event.

But Julee and her family didn't have a year. Not long ago, a radiologist told Julee and her husband, Bill, that time was running out. The cancer that had lived in her brain for seven years was on the move again. And it was moving quickly. "If you want to be part of your daughter's wedding," he advised, "make it happen now."

Three weeks later, without an invitation mailed, four hundred people gathered to celebrate the union of a handsome young couple—and pay loving tribute to a woman who is living by God's clock.

Just another story of family tragedy? Not in the least! I want to tell their story. I want you to sit in Julee's living room with me—not to mourn, but to witness in one woman's eyes something grander than the clock and to be touched by something as awe inspiring as grace.

"Pam, I'm sorry I have to close my eyes when I'm talking to you," Julee says, settling back in her pillow. "But looking at you makes me sick."

It's a typical Julee wordplay. She chuckles and I join in, even though the nausea caused by the pressure of the tumor on the optical nerve is no laughing matter. Today, as usual, it's the patient, not the counselor, whose sense of humor reaches out to comfort and heal.

Julee and Bill have been married for twenty-six years. Sparks first ignited between them during a backyard barbecue at a mutual friend's home in Covina. That afternoon, Jim was just back from Vietnam, and Julee was a gorgeous, blue-eyed blonde who stopped him in his tracks. Nine months later they were husband and wife.

Bill pursued a career in the printing industry, and he and Julee enjoyed raising their children, Levi and Merry. For decades they faced nothing besides the normal ups and downs of family life, and not many of those. In fact, Bill and Julee seemed to live a favored existence. Then came the moment seven years ago in Julee's optometrist's office. With one word, the couple heard for the first time, they say, the second hand ticking on God's clock.

"Tumor? What do you mean, tumor?" Julee asked, more puzzled than afraid. "I don't do tumors. Those are for *Readers Digest* stories," she told the optometrist. But Julee hadn't been feeling quite like herself for a couple of months. There had been headaches, moments of disorientation, and a fainting spell in the shower. A nurse had said her body was probably just overheated and had given her an antibiotic.

After the optometrist explained the reasons for his concern, Julee responded with characteristic wit: "Doctor, a brain tumor is just about the last thing that entered my mind!"

This office visit led to a CAT scan. Test results revealed a tumor three quarters the size of a tennis ball on the right frontal lobe of her brain. Julee met with a neurosurgeon the next day. "I expected to walk into a big office with a silver-haired, Marcus Welby-type doctor sitting behind his desk," she told me. "You know—the kind with deep age crinkles in his face from years of experience. Instead, I found myself greeted by a young doctor with a Southern drawl that wrapped a twang around every word."

Despite his folksy accent, the doctor was frank and to the point: "Mrs. Myers, this thing is going to kill you," he said. "All I can do is try to slow it down. We need to do a craniotomy and a right frontal lobectomy. You may not go home after the operation. You may not know who anyone is after surgery. You may lose your speech and be paralyzed on your left side. The only thing I can guarantee is that you will have two of the biggest black eyes you have ever seen."

A week later, following six hours of surgery, Julee woke up in the recovery room. As she slowly opened her eyes and began to focus, she saw a circle of faces looking down at her and asking, "Julee, can you hear me?" "Julee, can you move?" "Julee, can you talk?"

Much to the astonishment of the medical staff, Julee could do all those things. In fact, she soon proved there was no paralysis, no memory loss, no personality change—no impairment whatsoever from the surgical procedure. When the neurosurgeon walked into her room, he took one look at Julee and fluffed up like an old hen.

"Mrs. Myers! Where are your black eyes?" he blurted.

Julee looked on the side of her bed, under her pillow, beneath the covers, and then shrugged at the doctor. "Oh, dear," she whined, "did I do it wrong, Doc?"

"No, no, no," he reassured her.

"Phew!" Julee parried. "That's a load off of my mind!"

The doctor's medical efforts were far from completed. "Mrs. Myers, I'm going to recommend radiation treatment of your brain to try to kill the cancer," he explained. "The bad news is, the hair follicles will also be killed, and your hair will not grow back."

"Well, Doc, God has every hair on my head numbered," Julee replied. "I'm going to pray about this, and we'll just see what happens."

Seven weeks of radiation followed. The doctor was right about her hair falling out—but wrong about the rest. Julee's beautiful hair grew back—but rather creatively. Where the right frontal lobe had been removed, the hair grew in brown. The other three quarters of her hair came in her usual blond.

It wasn't until a year following her surgery that Julee collided for the first time with the specter of fear. She had been flipping through some of the hospital records about her cancer when her eyes fell upon the lab diagnosis of her cancer: anaplastic oligodendroglioma. The word *anaplastic* indicates a particularly aggressive and virulent form of cancer.

Through the previous twelve months, Julee had exuded calm

about her situation. But on this particular afternoon, her gloomy diagnosis, spelled out in cold, scientific terminology, stripped away her peace and triggered an avalanche of dread. Shaking, she grabbed her Bible, closed herself inside her closet, and sat on her pink stool for a heart-to-heart talk with God.

Opening to the book of John, she began reading chapter 6:

> [Jesus said,] "The Spirit gives life; the flesh counts for nothing. The words I have spoken to you are spirit and they are life. Yet there are some of you who do not believe."
>
> From this time many of his disciples turned back and no longer followed him.
>
> "You do not want to leave too, do you?" Jesus asked the Twelve.
>
> Simon Peter answered him, "Lord, to whom shall we go? You have the words of eternal life. We believe and know that you are the Holy One of God." (John 6:63–64, 66–68)

As she sorted through her feelings with the Lord, Julee began to reach some bottom-line convictions that day. In fact, she emerged from the closet with them written down and forged in the tempered steel of her spirit. She recited them to me seven years later with a clarity and a passion that I rarely see among those faced with adversity.

Here is what she wrote:

- Circumstances may change. Information from the doctors may change. But God will never change.
- Either I believe every word God says, or I believe none of it.
- The buck stops with God. There is no higher authority in my life.
- If I have truly entrusted my life to God, then how, when, or why I die is really none of my business.
- I will not die one minute before or one minute after God wants to take me home. So I'm not going to waste my energies fretting.
- God has promised me that He will complete the good work He began in me. My death will be an indication that He has finished His work, and accomplished His plan.

With those determinations in hand, Julee and Bill walked through the next years with heads up, tears flowing, and spirits firm. They endured all the roller-coaster rides of treatment with courage—even when, seemingly without warning, the clock started ticking again. Seven months ago, a new tumor was discovered at the base of Julee's brain stem. Seventeen surgeries have followed in quick succession, along with chemotherapy. Julee has clung stoutheartedly to her bottom-line convictions through it all—through discomfort, side effects, hospitalizations, blood clots, and a leaking spinal tap.

—⁂—

"I'm preparing for my graduation," Julee tells me today with a slight lilt in her voice. She doesn't look like Julee anymore. Though a size-eight beauty all of her life, the steroids used to treat the cancer induced a dramatic weight gain. She has ballooned to a size twenty-two.

But character always communicates a more profound message than cosmetics.

Today Julee glances upward. "I win!" she declares with conviction. "I'm going to get rid of this body!" Anticipation brings a smile to her face.

Merry's wedding last week, such a gift of God's love to the family, was only one sign of God's sovereign provision for Julee during her last days. Another smaller but more intimate provision is Sonjia. She is a regular by Julee's bedside. She also happens to be an old high-school friend of Julee's. You could say she's living evidence of "what goes around, comes around."

Julee tells me how they first met. Fourteen-year-old Sonjia was a casualty of multiple divorces who was handed off from one home to another. One Sunday morning when Sonjia was walking to the library, she passed a local church. Something told her to go inside. She'd never been to the church before and didn't know anyone. But on a whim she followed the prompting and slipped into a pew in the sanctuary. At the end of the preacher's message, Sonjia responded to his invitation to come forward for prayer. The warmhearted woman who prayed with her—and led her in the steps to salvation—was Julee's mother.

Thirty years later, through an odd twist of events, Sonjia is not only a neurosurgical nurse who specializes in brain tumors, but she is also the director of hospice care in a nearby city. She has been at Julee's side, answering the questions about the physical aspects of the dying process, helping to reduce the fear of the unknown. Sonjia's sweet presence reminds Julee daily that God hasn't lost track of her and that He is intimately acquainted with every detail of her journey. As Julee put it, "My mom introduced Sonjia to eternal life, and now Sonjia is helping escort me into eternity."

You feel a solemn reverence when you're in the presence of one who is standing at the edge of eternity. Heaven seems so close. Today as she reminisces, Julee sees eternity breaking through those joyful covenant moments at the altar. The wedding photographs remind her of how God graced her with the strength to participate in the celebration—almost as if the tumor didn't exist, she says. But the friends and family knew that it was, in many ways, a double ceremony: a welcome into a loving family for the new couple and a final good-bye for Mother.

As far as I can tell, the family thought the unusual wedding-and-farewell seemed a perfectly natural thing to do. When I ask her about it, Julee replies, "I think that we learn how to live by learning how to die." Then she points to her kitchen. "You see that tea kettle simmering on the stove? If I were to lift the lid for a quick second and then replace it, you'd see a brief shot of steam appear and then disappear."

I nod.

"That's how life is in this world. It's just like a vapor. The more I look at what I'm enduring in light of eternity, the smaller it all seems."

Julee doesn't know exactly when she will make that transition. But if she leaves her loved ones today, she believes it's only for a little while—just a brief pause in the eternal scheme of things. The rest of her family and friends will join her in good time, according to the appointed schedule.

Unimaginable suffering, unbelievable courage, and unshakable faith: that's Julee's legacy.

Julee settles deeper into her pillows. The room is quiet, so quiet I think I can hear the ticking of God's clock. But in this room it sounds more like the pulse of His heart—He who is our God of all comfort.

As I rise to leave, I feel as if I am standing on sacred ground. Julee's eyes follow me.

"The best is yet to come," she whispers.

Power Perks: A SIP OF HOPE AND HUMOR

There was a woman who had been diagnosed with a terminal illness and had been given three months to live. As she was getting her things in order, she asked her pastor to come to her house so they could discuss certain aspects of her final wishes. When he arrived, she told him which songs she wanted sung at the service, which Scriptures she would like read, and which outfit she wanted to be buried in along with her favorite Bible.

Everything was in order, and the pastor was preparing to leave when the woman suddenly remembered something very important to her. "There's one more thing!" she said excitedly.

"What's that?" asked the pastor.

"This is very important," the woman said. "I want to be buried with a fork in my right hand."

The pastor stood looking at the woman, not knowing quite what to say.

"That surprises you, doesn't it?" the woman asked.

"Well, to be honest, I'm puzzled by the request," said the pastor.

The woman explained. "In all my years of attending church socials and potluck dinners, I remember that when the dishes of the main course were being cleared, someone would inevitably lean over and say, 'Keep your fork.' It was my favorite part because I knew that something better was coming, like velvety chocolate cake or deep-dish apple pie. So I just want people to see me in my casket with a fork in my hand, and I want them to wonder about it. And I want you to tell them: 'Keep your fork—the best is yet to come.'"

The pastor's eyes welled up with tears of joy as he hugged the woman. He knew this would be one of the last times he would see her before her death.

At the funeral, people walking by the woman's casket saw the pretty dress she was wearing and her favorite Bible and the fork placed in her right hand. Over and over the pastor heard the question, "What's with the fork?" And over and over he smiled and told the people of the conversation he had with the woman shortly before she died—about the fork and what it symbolized to her.

The next time you see a fork, let it be a gentle reminder. The best is yet to come.

The created world is but a small parenthesis in eternity.

Sir Thomas Brown[1]

The Promised Land always lies on the other side of the wilderness.

Havelock Ellis[2]

Koffee Klatch Questions

I have designed the following questions for worn-out women who want to talk through the joys and challenges of life with their friends—preferably over coffee! Groups of two to six trusted women can create stimulating discussion and personal growth. Knowing we are not alone and hearing how others manage tough circumstances is empowering. I encourage you to be open and honest and to pray for one another. Strive for authenticity and meet regularly—and share more than great espresso. As you bear one another's burdens, watch the healing flow.

CHAPTER 1: A REMINDER TO REMEMBER

1. Can you call to mind an incident from your past when God intervened and made a difference in your daily life? Tell the group about it.

2. We build our faith by banking on what we know instead of ruminating on the unknown. What do you plan to do today to remind yourself of God's faithfulness to you in the past? Be sure to make your goal concrete and measurable.

CHAPTER 2: SOLITARY SPRINGS

1. What condition is your soul in today—harried or peaceful? What has contributed to that condition?

2. What do you do to replenish your cup when it's empty? Set a specific goal for the week and ask your group to hold you accountable.

CHAPTER 3: THE GIFT OF FAITH

1. Can you identify a fear that you are struggling with at this time in your life?

2. What are some faith statements that you can assertively direct toward those fears the next time they surface?

CHAPTER 4: SEASONS OF CHANGE

1. Share a time in your life when circumstances left you feeling pruned back to a stump.

2. As a result of that painful period, what evidences of fruitfulness do you enjoy now?

CHAPTER 5: SOWING HOPE'S SEEDS

1. In what ways do you need God to provide for you this week?

2. Can you think of a time when God has provided for you in the past? Please share the story with your group.

CHAPTER 6: A FRESH TOUCH

1. What do you turn to when your soul is feeling empty?

2. What specific goal can you set this week that will allow you to spend more time alone with your heavenly Father?

CHAPTER 7: POOPED OUT BY PERFECTIONISM

1. In what ways can you identify with Marti's struggles?
2. In what ways do you give yourself and others permission to fail, or to be less than perfect?

CHAPTER 8: WHAT AN INHERITANCE!

1. What character qualities would you like people to see in you? Ask your group to pray with you about this.
2. Can you think of some tangible ways to display those qualities during your interactions with others this week?

CHAPTER 9: THE POWER OF PERCOLATING PRAYERS

1. God never wastes the pain we suffer. He will always use it for our highest good. What good has come from something painful in your life?
2. What is one heartache you are experiencing during this season of your life? Allow your group members to pray for you.

CHAPTER 10: BICKERS AND BLUNDERS

1. What kinds of silly thoughts sneak up on you and grab you from behind when you are fatigued?
2. How do you typically handle conflict? Are you an internalizer or an externalizer? How does this compare with others in your family?

CHAPTER 11: A LONGING FOR SOMETHING MORE

1. Have you ever experienced a longing for something more? Talk about the related thoughts and feelings with your group.
2. Do you know your place in God's plan? If you don't, share ideas in your group about how you can begin to discover it. Pray about it together.

CHAPTER 12: BUGS IN THE BREW

1. How do you typically react when criticized? What do you think and feel?

2. How might living your life for an audience of One make a difference in your life this week?

CHAPTER 13: SHAPED FOR A HIGHER PURPOSE

1. Share with your group a difficult reality that you are trying to accept.

2. How have some of the difficulties you have endured shaped who you are today?

CHAPTER 14: WHEN YOU ARE AT WIT'S END CORNER

1. Is there an area of your life in which you feel you are at your wit's end? Explain.

2. Ask your group to help you brainstorm some options for getting around the corner and to Prosperity Drive. Select one option, and take a step in that direction today.

CHAPTER 15: THE ROAD TAKEN

1. "Worn-out women are sitting targets." On a scale of one to ten, how vulnerable are you to emotional or physical infidelity? Why?

2. "We can't have it all or do it all—at once." What tough choices have you made, or do you need to make, to maintain balance and live according to your convictions?

CHAPTER 16: CONSULT THE EXPERT

1. Can you recall a time when God led you to make a decision that has obviously worked for your highest good?

2. Can you recall ever making a big decision when you didn't consult the Expert? How did things turn out?

CHAPTER 17: FORGIVENESS IS SUPERNATURAL

1. Is there someone you need to forgive? If so, can you talk discreetly about the situation with the others in your group and ask them to pray for you?

2. Share about a time in your life when you forgave another and the results of doing so.

CHAPTER 18: CHRISTMAS CHAOS

1. What are some of your favorite past or present holiday traditions?

2. Flexibility and reassessing our expectations can diffuse stress in our lives. How can you apply these principles to your life this week?

CHAPTER 19: GOD'S MATH

1. What is one way you plan to give of yourself this week to make a difference in the life of another?

2. What assignments are draining you dry? Ask those in your small group to pray for you and to share insights that might help refill your cup.

CHAPTER 20: LIVING BY GOD'S CLOCK

1. Julee shared several of her deepest convictions in this story. Which of those convictions challenged you? Why?

2. Read James 4:13–15. Then answer this question: If you were told you had only a year to live, what changes would you make in the way you are living?

Notes

CHAPTER ONE

1. I have adapted these questions from Alan D. Wright, *The God Moment Principle* (Sisters, Ore.: Multnomah Publishers, 1999), 14.

2. Ibid.

3. Charles Spurgeon, *Morning and Evening* (Peabody, Mass.: Hendrickson Publishers, 1991), 382.

4. Edyth Draper, *Draper's Book of Quotations for the Christian World* (Wheaton, Ill.: Tyndale House, 1992), entry 7731.

CHAPTER TWO

1. Nelson Lin quoted in *Meet Me for Coffee* (Eugene, Ore.: Harvest House Publishers, 1998), 31.

2. Edyth Draper, *Draper's Book of Quotations for the Christian World* (Wheaton, Ill.: Tyndale House, 1992), entry 7710.

3. Ibid., entry 7711.

CHAPTER THREE

1. "Matthew Henry's Commentary on Matthew 8:5–13," in the *PC Study Bible Complete Reference Library* (Seattle: Biblesoft, 1992), 24.

2. My thanks to my mentor, Dr. Pamela Reeve, who has helped me develop my faith language through our times together and through her book, *Faith Is...* (Sisters, Ore: Multnomah Publishers, 1977).

3. Edyth Draper, *Draper's Book of Quotations for the Christian World* (Wheaton, Ill.: Tyndale House, 1992), entry 3640.

4. Ibid., entry 3651.

5. Ibid., entry 3693.

CHAPTER FOUR

1. Edyth Draper, *Draper's Book of Quotations for the Christian World* (Wheaton, Ill.: Tyndale House, 1992), entry 970.

CHAPTER FIVE

1. Dr. James Dobson, *Straight Talk to Men and Their Wives* (Waco, Tex.: Word Books, 1980), 96.

2. Edyth Draper, *Draper's Book of Quotations for the Christian World* (Wheaton, Ill.: Tyndale House, 1992), entry 3723.

3. Ibid., entry 3804.

4. Ibid., entry 3815.

CHAPTER SIX

1. Edyth Draper, *Draper's Book of Quotations for the Christian World* (Wheaton, Ill.: Tyndale House, 1992), entry 4296.

2. Ibid., entry 3918.

CHAPTER SEVEN

1. T. S. Eliot quoted in *Meet Me for Coffee* (Eugene, Ore.: Harvest House Publishers, 1998), 11.

2. Edyth Draper, *Draper's Book of Quotations for the Christian World* (Wheaton, Ill.: Tyndale House, 1992), entry 8519.

3. Ibid., entry 8523.

Chapter Eight

1. Philip G. Hamerton quoted in *Meet Me for Coffee* (Eugene, Ore.: Harvest House Publishers, 1998), 17.
2. Edyth Draper, *Draper's Book of Quotations for the Christian World* (Wheaton, Ill.: Tyndale House, 1992), entry 2068.
3. Ibid., entry 2073.
4. Ibid., entry 2056.
5. Ibid., entry 6246.

Chapter Nine

1. Edyth Draper, *Draper's Book of Quotations for the Christian World* (Wheaton, Ill.: Tyndale House, 1992), entry 929.
2. L. B. Cowman, *Streams in the Desert* (Grand Rapids, Mich.: Zondervan Publishing House, 1997), 134–135.

Chapter Ten

1. Edyth Draper, *Draper's Book of Quotations for the Christian World* (Wheaton, Ill.: Tyndale House, 1992), entry 1632.
2. Ibid., entry 4104.
3. Ibid., entry 5226.

Chapter Eleven

1. Edyth Draper, *Draper's Book of Quotations for the Christian World* (Wheaton, Ill.: Tyndale House, 1992), entry 312.
2. Ibid., entry 1139.
3. Ibid., entry 5908.

CHAPTER TWELVE

1. Edyth Draper, *Draper's Book of Quotations for the Christian World* (Wheaton, Ill.: Tyndale House, 1992), entry 2177.
2. Ibid., entry 2892.
3. Ibid., entry 5165.

CHAPTER THIRTEEN

1. Edyth Draper, *Draper's Book of Quotations for the Christian World* (Wheaton, Ill.: Tyndale House, 1992), entry 3707.
2. Ibid., entry 9229.
3. Ibid., entry 4559.

CHAPTER FOURTEEN

1. Edyth Draper, *Draper's Book of Quotations for the Christian World* (Wheaton, Ill.: Tyndale House, 1992), entry 289.
2. Ibid., entry 302.

CHAPTER FIFTEEN

1. Anne Morrow Lindbergh, *Gift from the Sea* (New York: Pantheon Books, 1955), 23–24.
2. Edyth Draper, *Draper's Book of Quotations for the Christian World* (Wheaton, Ill.: Tyndale House, 1992), entry 1141.
3. Ibid., entry 1145
4. Ibid., entry 1149.

CHAPTER SIXTEEN
1. Edyth Draper, *Draper's Book of Quotations for the Christian World* (Wheaton, Ill.: Tyndale House, 1992), entry 5399.
2. Ibid., entry 5455.
3. Ibid., entry 5468.

CHAPTER SEVENTEEN
1. Edyth Draper, *Draper's Book of Quotations for the Christian World* (Wheaton, Ill.: Tyndale House, 1992), entry 4078.
2. Ibid., entry 4072

CHAPTER EIGHTEEN
1. Edyth Draper, *Draper's Book of Quotations for the Christian World* (Wheaton, Ill.: Tyndale House, 1992), entry 4055.
2. Ibid., entry 1366.
3. Ibid., entry 1369.
4. Ibid., entry 1361.
5. Ibid., entry 971.

CHAPTER NINETEEN
1. Edyth Draper, *Draper's Book of Quotations for the Christian World* (Wheaton, Ill.: Tyndale House, 1992), entry 9.
2. Ibid., entry 7350.
3. Ibid., entry 154.

CHAPTER TWENTY
1. Edyth Draper, *Draper's Book of Quotations for the Christian World* (Wheaton, Ill.: Tyndale House, 1992), entry 3284.
2. Ibid., entry 5669.

Do You Know Anyone Who Is a Pooped Out Parent?

ISBN 1-57673-485-4

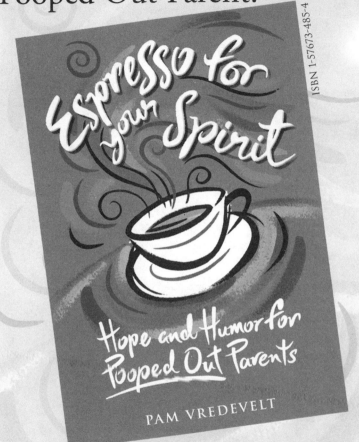

...one more dirty diaper, bloody knee, or soccer team fund-raiser and you'll scream! When it feels like you're stringing beads with no knot at the end, you need a steaming cup of reassurance and hope—and a warm reminder that God is mightily at work in your family.

BOOKS BY
PAM VREDEVELT

To schedule Pam Vredevelt for conference speaking, you
may write: Pam Vredevelt (Conference), P.O. Box 1093,
Gresham, OR 97030

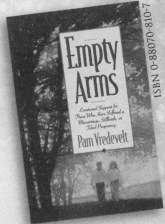

ISBN 0-88070-810-7

EMPTY ARMS:
*Emotional Support for Those
Who Have Suffered a Miscarriage,
Stillbirth, or Tubal Pregnancy*

ISBN 1-57673-250-9

ANGEL BEHIND THE ROCKING CHAIR
In these stories of hope and encouragement, share in the blessings and heartache
that come with having a Down's syndrome
child. Walk with families that face
unexpected adversities, revealing how
in the imperfections of our lives, God's
perfect glory shines through.

OTHER BOOKS

Mothers and Sons: Raising Boys to Be Men (with Jean Lush)
Women and Stress (with Jean Lush)
The Thin Disguise: Understanding and Overcoming Anorexia and Bulimia
(with Dr. Frank Minirth, Dr. Debra Newman, and Harry Beverly)